The
Healthy
Exchanges®
Diabetic Desserts
Cookbook

M000277155

Also by Joanna M. Lund:

The Open Road Cookbook
Cooking Healthy With a Man in Mind
String of Pearls
Cooking Healthy Across America
Cooking Healthy With the Kids in Mind
A Potful of Recipes
Healthy Exchanges Cookbook
The Heart Smart Healthy Exchanges Cookbook
The Arthritis Healthy Exchanges Cookbook
The Strong Bones Healthy Exchanges Cookbook
The Diabetics Healthy Exchanges Cookbook

Most Perigee Books are available at special quantity discounts for bulk purchases for sales promotions, premiums, fund-raising or educational use. Special books, or book excerpts, can also be created to fit specific needs.

For details, write: Special Markets, The Berkley Publishing Group, 375 Hudson Street, New York, New York 10014.

The Healthy Exchanges® Diabetic Desserts Cookbook

JoAnna M. Lund

with
Barbara Alpert

Portions of this book were previously published in *Dessert Every Night!*

A Perigee Book

A Perigee Book
Published by The Berkley Publishing Group
A division of Penguin Group (USA) Inc.
375 Hudson Street
New York, New York 10014

Copyright © 2003 by Healthy Exchanges, Inc.
Cover photo copyright © 1998 by Zeva Oelbaum
Food stylist: Jennifer Udell
Cover photo of the author by Glamour Shots® of Des Moines

Diabetic Exchanges calculated by Rose Hoenig, R.D., L.D.

For more information about Healthy Exchanges products, contact:
Healthy Exchanges, Inc.
P.O. Box 80
DeWitt, Iowa 52742-0124
(563) 659-8234

Portions of this book were previously published in *Dessert Every Night!*
First edition: May 2003

Library of Congress Cataloging-in-Publication Data

Lund, JoAnna M.
    The Healthy Exchanges diabetic desserts cookbook / JoAnna M. Lund, with Barbara Alpert.
       p. cm.
    Includes index.
    ISBN 0-399-52884-9
    1. Diabetes—Diet therapy—Recipes. 2. Desserts. I. Alpert, Barbara. II. Healthy Exchanges, Inc. III. Title.

RC662.L863 2003
641.5'6314—dc21

                                                                        2002045026

Printed in the United States of America

10 9 8 7 6 5 4 3 2 1

This cookbook, as all my books are, is dedicated in loving memory to my parents, Jerome and Agnes McAndrews. As sure as the sun rose in the morning, we could be positive that Mom would be stirring up a delectable dessert to serve to us that evening. Sometimes her desserts were "recycled" leftovers, such as rice or bread pudding. Other times our dessert might be a scrumptious strawberry shortcake, made with berries picked fresh from her patch. And still other times we would be presented with a magnificent cake *almost* too pretty to cut. Each and every day was a reason to celebrate with dessert.

I don't know who loved those desserts more, us kids and Daddy, as we savored every bite, or Mom, as she lovingly prepared them to share with her family. But I do know that I developed a love for dessert at an early age. I'm proud to share with you and your family the types of desserts my mother so proudly shared with us. I've kept the eye and mouth satisfaction she was so famous for, but I've taken my "magic wire whisk" and whisked out the excess fats, sugars, calories, sodium, and cost—while whisking in flavor, ease of preparation, and health! After just a bite of any of these tasty treats, I think you, too, will agree that *diet* and *dessert* are indeed in the same *D* section of the dictionary . . . and not with *dull* and *dreadful*, but with *delightful* and *delicious*!

My mother had a poem that almost seems as though she wrote it knowing that, years later, I would share it with you in this dessert cookbook. While Mom was speaking about the beauty of nature, she applied those same ideas to her desserts . . . especially how little touches make a big difference.

A Poet Speaks

If I were a gifted artist and painted
    night and day,
I could never capture the exquisiteness
    of April or May.
I wish I could paint this scenery that is
    now all around.
Every tree, bush and flower is dressed
    in its party gown.
The lilac bush is elegant with plumes
    of purple and white,
While the fruit and magnolia trees are truly
    a heavenly sight.
Grass is an emerald carpet embossed with lit-
    tle golden dots,
While beds of daffodils are edged with tiny
    forget-me-nots.
Gardens are perfumed with blossoms in rain-
    bow colors of every hue.
And woodlands are sprinkled with wild ones
    translucent, yellow and blue.
I would also add fresh black soil
    from fields of Iowa sod
Then, title this beautiful picture
    The Miracle of God.
                —*Agnes Carrington McAndrews*

Contents

Acknowledgments

I firmly believe that a day without dessert is like a day without sunshine. And that sun is going to shine every day of my life! For helping me share the "desserts and sunshine" of my work with others, I want to thank:

John Duff, my editor. That first day, when he licked his plate clean after trying Triple Layer Party Pie, I *knew* we would get along.

Angela Miller and Coleen O'Shea, my agents. At our first meeting, I served them Blueberry Mountain Cheesecake. Just one minute and one bite later, they asked to represent me.

Barbara Alpert, my writing partner. When she came to Iowa for her first visit, I had Orange Chocolate Crumb Cheesecake waiting for her. We've been working together ever since!

Shirley Morrow, my typist. After a long evening of typing recipes, I shared a piece of Ruby Rhubarb Cheesecake with her. She remarked that it more than made up for all my misspelled words.

Rita Ahlers, my recipe tester. She thought every day she was testing was "party time," but the afternoon Rita stirred up Hawaiian Paradise Cheesecake, she declared she was in Pie Paradise!

Rose Hoenig, R.D., L.D., my dietetic consultant. She's written that healthy food isn't "Pie in the Sky" when it comes to a Healthy Exchanges recipe. She's especially fond of Pretty in Pink Cake, the dessert she chose to share at her mother's birthday party.

Becky and John Taylor, James and Pam Dierickx, and Tom and Angie Dierickx, my children. They've always had their favorites— Becky and John love Old-Fashioned Cherry Cheesecake; James and Pam are partial to Cherry Kolaches; and Tom and Angie go for French Pear Cream Pie. But they are *always* willing to try new creations.

Zach, Josh, Aaron and Abram Dierickx; Cheyanne and Camryn Dierickx; Spencer and Ellie Taylor, my beloved grandchildren. When they chime in together, "Pie, Grandma, pie," it's music to my ears. So far, their "most favorite" is Better Than Candy Pie. But that's subject to change the next time we get to share both yummy dessert and precious time together.

Cliff Lund, my husband and business partner. He's said more than once that the best part of his job is being the Official Taste Tester of Healthy Exchanges. I don't think he's ever enjoyed his duties more than when he had to try Banana Split Pie.

God, my creator. When I was given the gift of stirring up "common folk" healthy recipes, He doubly blessed me when it came to desserts. I plan on sharing many more of those desserts until the day I hope to start specializing in angel food cake in "Cookbook Heaven"!

Pre-Diabetes:
What You Should Know

Pre-diabetes could be called the 'tween stage—that's between not having and having diabetes. Before March 2002 this 'tween stage was known in the medical community as either impaired glucose tolerance (IGT) or impaired fasting glucose (IFG). The new term, pre-diabetes, is used to describe the increasingly common condition in which blood glucose levels are higher than normal, but not yet high enough to be diagnostic for diabetics.

According to Dr. Francine Kaufman, an endocrinologist and president of the American Diabetes Association, "This new recommendation gives physicians added incentive to screen their middle-aged, overweight patients for both Type II diabetes or pre-diabetes. If you have pre-diabetes, you need to know it. Then you can learn about the high risk of getting diabetes and the steps you can take to prevent it. If you already have Type II diabetes, you need to be treated early to prevent complications." It is estimated that about 17 million Americans have diabetes. Unfortunately nearly 6 million of these people have not yet been diagnosed or learned how to manage their Type II diabetes. And now it is estimated that another 16 million have pre-diabetes. The table following shows you the blood glucose levels for normal, pre-diabetes and diabetes.

	Normal Plasma Glucose Levels	Pre Diabetes^ Glucose Levels	Diabetes* Glucose Levels
Fasting	< 110 mg/dl	≥110 and < 126 mg/dl	≥ 126
2 hours after eating a large amount of glucose	< 140 mg/dl	≥ 140 and < 200 mg/dl	≥ 200 mg/dl
Anytime			Symptoms of diabetes and casual plasma glucose ≥ 200 mg/dl

^It is more likely for a person with pre-diabetes and/or early onset Type II diabetes to have a normal fasting plasma glucose but a higher than normal 2-hour glucose level.

*A diagnosis of diabetes has to be confirmed on a subsequent day by measuring a fasting plasma glucose, 2 hours after eating or casual (any time of day) plasma glucose.

Legend.
    < less than
    - equal to
    > higher than or greater than

What Are the Risks?

The same people who are at risk for Type II diabetes are at risk for pre-diabetes. The following are considered the risk factors:

- a fasting and/or after eating blood glucose level that is higher than normal

- a sibling or parent who has or had diabetes

- a body mass index (BMI) of greater than 25

- a triglyceride level equal to or higher than 250

- a high-density lipoprotein level (good cholesterol) equal to or less than 35

- high blood pressure equal to or higher than 140/90

- physically inactive

- over 45 years of age

- members of ethnic groups that have greater than average incidences of diabetes: African American, Hispanic American, American Indian, Asian American and Pacific Islander

- gestational (during pregnancy) diabetes or having a baby or babies weighing more than 9 pounds

How Can You Find Out if You Have Diabetes?

If you have one or more of the risk factors for pre-diabetes, let your health care provider know now. Then ask them to check your blood glucose level. The blood glucose level that best detects pre-diabetes is a 2-hour oral glucose tolerance test. That's because the most common problem in pre-diabetes and early onset Type II diabetes is inability of the pancreas to put out insulin immediately after food is eaten. So fasting blood glucose levels may be normal, but after-meal blood glucose levels may be abnormal. Your health care provider can start by checking a casual blood glucose level, meaning any time of the day. If it is higher than normal, this is an indicator you have pre-diabetes or Type II diabetes. It tells you that you and your health care provider should investigate this situation further and do more blood glucose testing.

If you find out your blood glucose level is in the normal range and you don't have risk factors for Type II diabetes or pre-diabetes and you are over forty-five years old, then get your blood glucose level checked again in three years. However, if you have risk factors for pre-diabetes or Type I diabetes, then it is wise to get your blood glucose level checked each year.

What can you do about pre-diabetes?

If you have pre-diabetes or are at risk for it, there are several steps you can take. First, if you are carrying around extra pounds, try to shed a few of them. It has been shown in people with pre-diabetes that even a small weight loss (7 percent) and doing at least 150 minutes of activity per week (30 minutes, 5 times per week) reduces blood glucose levels, improves blood lipids and lowers blood pressure. With these simple steps, you can significantly increase your chances of preventing and/or delaying the development of diabetes as well as improving your health in general.

At this time, the American Diabetes Association does not recommend any diabetes medication for people with pre-diabetes. In fact, in a recent large study, the Diabetes Prevention Program, weight loss and increasing activity were more successful at preventing the onset of diabetes than the use of a diabetes medication such as metformin/Glucophage.

But . . . I Love Desserts!

Does having pre-diabetes mean having to give up desserts? Absolutely not! Today people with diabetes don't even have to give up desserts. That's because it is no longer believed that sugars and sweets raise blood glucose higher or more quickly than other sources of carbohydrate, such as bread, pasta or beans. But that doesn't mean merrily eat lots of sugars and sweets!

Due to general health concerns and to the calories in sugars and sweets, you still need to limit them. Bottom line, you need to include sugars and sweets in an eating plan that is both satisfying and that allows you to achieve your nutrition goals. One way to do this is to learn to make healthier desserts. And JoAnna Lund helps you do just that with the dessert recipes in this book.

Hope S. Warshaw, MMSc, RD, CDE
Diabetes Educator and Freelance Writer,
author of *The Diabetes Food and Nutrition Bible* and *Guide to Healthy Restaurant Eating*

Putting Dessert
on the Menu

Have you ever heard the slogan "Life is uncertain, eat dessert first"? It always gets a smile, and for a moment people think, sure, that would be fun, eating pie before the pot roast. But underneath that lighthearted motto is a kind of unexpressed fear: that something unexpected might happen—and they'll miss dessert!

I've often thought that the people who laugh the loudest and smile the widest may be the people for whom this concern is often reality, but not because life is uncertain. Instead, they miss dessert because they're dieting, or they're diabetic, or they have heart disease or high cholesterol. They know what it's like to skip dessert, how it makes life less pleasurable to do without what they enjoy.

I know what they're feeling, because I've shared that sense of deprivation. But I decided that I couldn't live that way for a lifetime. So I found a way of life that not only "lets" me have dessert, it's practically a requirement! My secret was, and is, Healthy Exchanges, where one thing's as certain as the sun rising every morning: DESSERT EVERY NIGHT!

When I talk to people all over the country who are struggling, often unsuccessfully, to lose weight and keep it off, or to regulate their blood sugar and keep it stable, or to lower their cholesterol and reduce their risk of heart disease, many begin by telling me they just don't have enough willpower to stick to a diet, or enough time to prepare healthy food.

But then, they often stop in midsentence and confess the real truth: "I just can't live without real dessert. I see a piece of pie or cake, or I smell fresh cookies baking, or everyone else is having ice cream—and all I can think about is how good it will taste. I have to have it."

1

I know that feeling.

It was one of the reasons I weighed 300 pounds in January 1991.

But when I finally decided to stop ignoring my own hunger for sweets and feed it instead, I lost 130 pounds—and have kept it off for more than ten years!

Why Giving Up Dessert Was Never the Answer

I used to be a professional dieter, losing and gaining weight as the seasons changed. But even when I gave up all the fattening foods I loved, especially desserts, I remained a failure at keeping the weight off.

I felt deprived, miserable, starved for the sweet tastes I loved—but also starved for the warmth and love that desserts represented to me. My mother was a wonderful cook and baker, and I learned my love of cooking and food in her kitchen, watching her roll out dough for her cherry kolaches, and counting the minutes until dinner ended and her delicious home-baked dessert was served.

In fact, dessert was like the period at the end of a sentence: it was just a given that dessert would be served at the end of a meal. We weren't a demonstrative family; there were few obvious shows of affection, but we knew we were loved and wanted. My mother showed her love in many ways, but like so many women of her generation, she particularly expressed her love with food.

And while all of her food spelled love to us, her desserts—gelatin desserts, cakes, kolaches fresh from the oven—drove the idea home! She made everything look so pretty, just like the dishes we saw in magazines or on television. We didn't have a lot of money, but there was always good food on the table, and it became natural for us to reach for food to make ourselves feel better.

Not every child experiences these emotions in the same way. My older sister, Mary, sat at the same table and ate the same food, but she never experienced a problem with her weight. She was always satisfied with one piece, while I often wanted more. My younger sister, Jeannie, didn't look to food for comfort, either. But I was the middle child, the peacemaker and the peacekeeper. Perhaps, in dealing with uncomfortable emotions, I found my solace in food.

I struggled for years, denying myself the foods I loved and the soothing comfort they provided. But no matter what I did, the weight never stayed off for long. In fact, my efforts often made the problem worse. I developed a dangerous habit of bingeing on cake doughnuts that lasted for a long time.

I can actually pinpoint when my obsession began. It was back in the spring of 1963, after I had gone on my first diet. I was drinking Metrecal, the first of the liquid diet drinks. I drank it every day for three weeks, and I lost ten pounds, but not off my behind, which is where I wanted to lose it all! Disappointed, I ended that diet, but instead of reverting to my generally good eating habits, which had kept me from having a weight problem during high school, I responded to my three weeks of complete deprivation by deciding I wasn't going to "go without" anymore!

The day after I went off that horrendous liquid diet, I gobbled down about half a dozen doughnuts in about an hour. I thought I was just going to eat one, but I kept going. I tried to rearrange the remaining doughnuts in the box so that no one would know what I'd done. Maybe because of the fast, or maybe just because I liked the taste, cake doughnuts became my binge food of choice—and to heck with the rest of the world! Like many people who eat this way, I devoured my doughnuts in private, sitting all by myself in the kitchen or later on in my car. I used to stuff the bags under the seat to keep my secret. I'd fish them out later and put them in the trash.

Eating with Emotion and with Memories

Those cake doughnuts, which I often smeared with butter, filled some kind of emotional need for me. Even though eating them became a kind of trap, I think I used them to feel loved. Butter was my favorite food from childhood, a treat that always reminded me of my father's love. And the doughnuts represented the kind of affection I used to feel from my mother when she cooked and baked for us.

It was only when I gave myself permission so many years later to enjoy my food, especially dessert, that I stopped sneaking it, inhaling it, and denying that I was consuming it! Dessert became my friend, not my enemy, and not my lover, either. That's when I started to come to terms with my weight, and with my health.

I finally understood what I hadn't seen before: that for me, dessert has always been connected with those cozy memories of my family seated around the table, sharing good food and the warmth of our love for each other. My memories of those times were as sweet as the pies and cakes and puddings that Mom prepared, and it took me a long time to recognize that I couldn't live the rest of my life denying my hunger for those good feelings.

When I finally decided to quit dieting and start living healthy, I promised my taste buds that I would have a real piece of a good dessert *every day*. I began creating hundreds of luscious dessert recipes of all kinds, each one more scrumptious than the last—and each one low in fat and sugar, but still truly satisfying to my eye as well as my tummy.

Eating dessert—and enjoying the good feelings that dessert gave me—helped me lose 130 pounds, and keep it off for over ten years now. By feeding my soul what I needed, I gave my body permission to let go of all those unwanted pounds once and for all.

Every one of the recipes in this book looks like a real treat, something you'd usually have to go off your diet to enjoy—a dish that is *worth* the anxiety of "cheating."

But here's the best part: with Healthy Exchanges, having your cake (or pie or brownie or other sweet treat) is a good-for-you splurge, one you can enjoy every single day if you choose—and still lose weight.

In fact, if your favorite "go-off-your-diet" binge has always been a banana split, I've got good news—I've created just about every kind of banana split dessert possible, from sweet salad to cream pie, from shortcake to cream cake, and I'm always coming up with more! Can you imagine having "permission" to enjoy the banana split you always had to gobble down in secret? Now, you *do*.

You see, people don't think *diet* and *dessert* are in the same *D* section of the dictionary, but they are—*if* they're Healthy Exchanges recipes. They're not with *dreadful* or *dull*, but with *delightful* and *delicious*.

It's time we stopped fearing special occasions and family gatherings because of the food, and instead planned for them. Preparing great-looking, great-tasting desserts that are designed to be part of a healthy lifestyle lets everyone interested in good health *and* good food be part of the party!

Sharing Your House with Dessert

Ever since I began sharing my recipes through my books and my newsletter, desserts have been the most beloved and popular food category with my Healthy Exchanges family members. They sent me beloved family favorites and requested that I make them over in a healthy way. They pleaded for more holiday cookies their children and friends could enjoy; they asked for recipes they could bring to family reunions and serve at birthday parties. They wondered if I could invent a healthy crumbly coffeecake (yes!) or a banana cream pie that would produce only feelings of pleasure, not guilt (yes again!).

But then I started getting mail and questions during my lectures about how to handle having all those luscious desserts in the house. "It calls to me from the refrigerator," one woman said with an embarrassed expression. "Last week I made one of your pies and truly enjoyed the piece I had for dessert after dinner. But that night, after everyone was sleeping, I slipped down to the kitchen and ate another piece. And then another one. I know it's a healthy pie, but I'm still binge eating."

She isn't alone in her concern. Many longtime dieters and binge eaters have told me that they love my entrees, but they just don't trust themselves with one of my pies. Instead of trying to figure out how to handle the problem, they continue the vicious cycle of deprivation, skipping dessert completely—and eventually they fall off the Health Wagon.

If this is a concern for you, it's time to face your fear—and finally put it to rest. The first time you make a Healthy Exchanges pie that serves eight, you may very well eat two pieces instead of just one. You may even eat three. It's because you still don't believe that you can have it, so you've got to gobble it up and get it out of the house so it doesn't tempt you.

But those days are over. You can have a piece of pie *every single day*. Maybe that should be your new mantra, chanted (under your breath if you prefer) whenever you feel that old behavior coming on. Right now, two rooms away from where I'm sitting, there are about ten different desserts that we made in the test kitchen today. I could walk in there now (the employees have all gone home), and I could eat a piece of every single one. Who would know? Only me. But I've already had my dinner, and I chose my one piece of dessert for tonight. I enjoyed every single bite, and I can still recall how good it tasted. That's all I'm going to have—and I'm okay with it.

Believe me, I didn't always feel this way. But I know that tomorrow, as sure as the sun rises, I'm going to have another piece of some kind of dessert. And the next day, too, and the one after that. Because I know that I can have more tomorrow, I can let the rest sit there on the counter without being afraid.

If you've deprived yourself of good-tasting desserts for a long time, you might struggle for a while controlling the urge to eat "the whole thing." But by the third or fourth time you stir up one of my pies, it'll click in—and you'll know what I know.

(Did anyone ever say to you, "If you're hungry, just eat an apple?" Was that person a skinny mini? Some people just don't understand that eating an apple only makes us hungrier. I'm no sooner finished, my taste buds are awakened, and I'm telling them the party's over. An apple is fine for a snack, but apple pie, that's dessert! Apple Crumb Pie, in fact—in the Pies section—does it for me!)

Please, JoAnna, May I Have Some More?

Many fans of Healthy Exchanges desserts have wondered if they may have more than one dessert a day. Is dessert at every meal a possibility? Here's how to think about this: When you look at a piece of pie or a dish of pudding, it looks like dessert. But it's also part of your daily menu of Food Exchanges. One piece might include exchanges from the Bread, Protein, Fruit, Vegetable, Skim Milk, and Fat groups as well as Optional Calories and Sliders (more about those later!).

So, yes, it's possible to enjoy dessert more than once a day—as long as you can stay within your allowance of exchanges, and as long as it's the accent to the meal, *not* the main course. The heart of Healthy Exchanges is good nutrition, and you never want to lose sight of that while planning your daily menu. That doesn't mean that every day needs to be the same. Sometimes I have a piece of dessert for breakfast, and I don't feel a bit guilty about it. I just don't do it every day. I'm living in the real world, and last time I checked my driver's license, it didn't say Saint JoAnna of Heaven, it said JoAnna Lund of DeWitt, Iowa. So—as long as I make sure that all my nutritional bases are covered, as long as I'm eating a reasonable amount of protein and veggies, as long as I'm getting my calcium, I've got the freedom to enjoy dessert in moderation . . . and whenever I choose.

I don't recommend having two pieces of dessert at one meal, in part because it distracts you from my suggested portion size. Also, you're likely cheating yourself of other good nutritional choices in order to fit those extra exchanges in. Your better bet is a lighter dessert at one meal, and a substantial one at another. I often have fruit for a snack, but I look forward to enjoying a piece of pie or cake after supper.

And—don't faint—I sometimes enjoy a dessert that isn't made from a Healthy Exchanges recipe! Remember, I live in the real world, I travel, and I attend all kinds of celebrations. I believe in picking your times and places, so I try never to waste my calories on anything but the best. (If it's special, if it rings your bells, if it's your sister's chocolate mousse wedding cake, of course you should taste it.) I never feel as if I've gone "off my diet" if I eat a piece of cheesecake or order bread pudding in a restaurant. And a few bites satisfy me, because I know it's not the last piece of cheesecake I'll ever eat.

Just remember this: Dessert is *not* one of the food groups. It's the exclamation point of living healthy, not the whole sentence.

Getting the Family to Climb on the Health Wagon with You

If the way to a man's heart is through his stomach, then the way to win your husband's heart and mind over to your new healthy lifestyle is probably to woo him with some of my Healthy Exchanges desserts! I know that they're man-pleasers because I have my own live-in taste tester in my husband, Cliff. A long-distance trucker who hauled industrial cargo until he quit trucking to "truck me around," Cliff takes his job as the chief Healthy Exchanges dessert tester very seriously! Without any prompting from me, he used to share my healthy pies with his trucking buddies, so I knew I was on the right track. (And don't for a second think that men don't pay attention to what you feed them. Ever since I began speaking on the radio about Healthy Exchanges, I've been hearing from men who wanted to try my desserts—and again from them after they tasted them!)

The same goes for bringing kids along for the ride. Dessert is one of the first things we learn to love as children, and more battles are waged over what kids might be eating when they're away from home. I think it's good to offer the tastiest possible healthy desserts at home, and show your kids that it's okay to enjoy their food. (If they hear you constantly saying, "Oh, I shouldn't eat that," but then you do, they won't take you seriously when you try to teach them good nutrition.) Sure, children will occasionally come home from a party with a sugar high from gobbling too much candy or cake and ice cream, but instead of overreacting, just compensate by making sure they're well nourished at the very next meal. By not making a big scene, you don't encourage your kids to sneak around. And you can show them how special they are with foods besides dessert. My children felt loved when I served them vegetable soup made extra-special with alphabet macaroni.

Where Do All Those Desserts Come From?

I get asked this a lot. Sometimes I create my delectable dessert recipes by watching a high-fat version go by in a restaurant and thinking about how I could make the same dish in a healthy way. Other times, the ideas for sweet treats come so fast and furiously my husband, Cliff, tells me he can see smoke coming out of my ears and out of my pen as I scribble them down—in the car, at the table, watching TV! I seem to go into another world where it's just me and the recipes. My grandbabies could be making noise, the radio could be on, all kinds of normal commotion might be going on that would distract most people. But until I'm through, I don't come back to the real world.

One time, I was having my picture taken when I suddenly got an idea for cappuccino rice pudding. I was so busy writing, they had to bring me back to reality *three* times to get me to move so they could adjust the light.

And the wheels are always turning. I had picked a friend up at the airport and was driving her to DeWitt when we got on the topic of bath gel and all the fragrances it comes in. She told me she liked one that was a combination of strawberry and kiwi and pineapple. All the time she was telling me about it, I was inventing a sweet salad that featured that combination of flavors.

One of my best-loved desserts was developed while we were driving in the van to a radio appearance in Youngstown, Ohio. As we passed through Gary, Indiana, a vision of what became Triple Layer Party Pie (featured in *The Healthy Exchanges Cookbook*) just flashed through my mind. Because I never leave home without my wire whisk, my dry milk powder, and my mixing bowl, I was able to make the pie in the ladies' room of the radio station, then serve it to the host fifteen minutes later. The show was *The Party Line*; the combination of chocolate, butterscotch, and creamy topping lets you have a party in your mouth; the dessert has three layers—so Triple Layer Party Pie was born!

A few years later, this recipe earned another name: "The Pie That Wowed New York." I served it to all the publishers I met with before becoming Putnam's newest cookbook author in 1994. Have whisk, will travel, I like to say. I whisk out the excess fats and sugars, and whisk in ease of preparation and lots of flavor!

I'm not kidding about ease of preparation, either. In fact, I could take my act to Vegas—JoAnna and her Magic Pies, I'd call it. When I stir up a pie, pour the filling into the crust, then turn it upside down thirty seconds later, *it's set.* I like to watch everyone's mouth drop to their knees. It really is magic!

One time, I did a television show in Toledo, and when I was booked, I'd promised to make a sinful-looking sinless cheesecake in three minutes flat. Just before the interview, their weatherman told me he was doing the spot with me, and he showed up with a stopwatch, saying, "We're going to time you, and see if you're as good as you say you are." He held up the watch for everyone to see, then started it as I began stirring my ingredients up. I fixed the cheesecake, poured it in the crust, garnished it, cut it, and served it to him—and exactly two minutes and six seconds had elapsed. He tasted it, checked his watch, and said, "Wow! You're even *better* than you said you were!" Then, after he took a bite, he added, "If I hadn't seen it with my own eyes, I wouldn't have believed it. This doesn't taste 'diet-y' or thrown together."

If you've always believed that the only good desserts are the traditional high-fat, high-sugar recipes you've eaten all your life, then any one of thousands of cookbooks will do. And if you're convinced that only fat-free, sugar-free, and calorie-free food is healthy and good for you, you'll have to settle for a "pine float."

What's that?

Why, it's a toothpick floating in a glass of water!

But if you're looking for delicious low-fat, low-sugar, low-calorie, and high-flavor ultraquick desserts, this is the book you've been dreaming about!

The Proof of the Pudding (or the Pie ...)

Some time ago, I shared a remarkable story in my newsletter about the role desserts can play in a healthy lifestyle.

A man came to my Healthy Exchanges Family Reunion Potluck Picnic, and told me that a year before, his triglycerides had been measured at 1,700. His doctor prescribed a low-fat diet along with niacin pills, and he succeeded in lowering his triglyceride levels first to 600, then 400. He was eating only 20 grams or less of fat a day, and really going overboard on the pasta and the bread. He'd been told to emphasize low-fat, high-volume foods.

Well, no matter how he tried, he just couldn't get his triglycerides below 400. Then he and his wife went on vacation and returned to find that his doctor had retired. He went to see a new doctor, who did blood tests and discovered he was also a Type II diabetic and needed to watch his carbs and sugars as well as fats.

He attended a class I gave at a local hospital, and purchased my book and newsletter. He raised his fat to 35 grams a day, and he began having a piece of healthy pie from my recipes *every single night*. (He counted it as one of his starches.) Well, he went back to his doctor less than a month later and found that his triglycerides were down to the 170s. His doctor asked, "What have you been doing?" He answered, "Eating healthy pie." The doctor shook his head and said, "Whatever works!"

The last time I saw him, he'd lost 35 pounds and his triglycerides were 177. This is a perfect example to show that desserts don't have to be unhealthy, and when used in the proper way, they're exceptionally good for you. I'm convinced it's because they feed the soul as well as the stomach.

Every Healthy Exchanges recipe is low in fat. But—and this is a really important "but"—*that's not all*. My recipes are also low in sugar, *and* portion controlled. So many people have jumped on the low-fat bandwagon without thinking clearly. They gobble down an entire box of fat-free cookies and still expect to lose weight. *You can't.* But you *can* enjoy healthy treats in *moderation* as part of your eating plan.

This book will highlight another important Healthy Exchanges principle: my serving sizes are *realistic*, not ridiculous. You get one-eighth of a Healthy Exchanges pie, not a skinny sliver that crumbles when you try to serve it. I'd never tell you that *one* cookie is a reasonable serving, either. You're entrusting your health to me, and I take that responsibility seriously. When I tell you that a dessert serving provides specific nutrients, I'm telling you that I've done the work for you, and all you have to do is enjoy. But I've discovered that not every health-oriented cookbook gives you the same guarantee. I picked up a diabetic cookbook recently in a bookstore and was shocked to see a pie that delivered a whopping 80 grams of carbohydrate and 20 grams of fat. Can you imagine what that would do to someone's blood sugar, not to mention his or her arteries? Then there was the diet cookbook that featured a Black Forest dessert. The numbers looked good—160 calories per serving, and 5 grams of fat. But then I looked at the serving size and gasped. This recipe, prepared in an 8-by-8-inch pan, served 32, instead of the usual 4 or 6 or 8 that my recipes do! I'd never call one bite a serving, and you shouldn't settle for such unrealistic recommendations.

My recipes have to satisfy the eye, the taste buds, and the emotional connection that dessert recalls. It's a big job, but my readers keep telling me that I'm succeeding. Once I decided that a day without dessert is like a day without sunshine, I knew what my mission would be! Someday, when I'm stirring up angel food cake in "Cookbook Heaven," I want my epitaph to read:

She shared HELP with the rest of the world, and
she created Hawaiian Strawberry Pie.

(I created this recipe back in 1992 for my Healthy Exchanges Food Newsletter, and it's remained my favorite through the creation of thousands of recipes since. Though my normal practice is not to repeat a recipe, I can't imagine publishing a dessert cookbook without including it—so here it is as a bonus. Just think of it as the sugar-free frosting on the delicious fat-free cake!)

Hawaiian Strawberry Pie

○ Serves 8

2 cups sliced fresh strawberries
1 (6-ounce) Keebler graham cracker piecrust
1 (4-serving) package JELL-O sugar-free strawberry gelatin
1 (4-serving) package JELL-O sugar-free vanilla cook-and-serve
*   pudding mix*
1 (8-ounce) can crushed pineapple, packed in fruit juice, drained,
*   and ¼ cup liquid reserved*
1¼ cups water
1 teaspoon coconut extract
1 cup Cool Whip Lite
2 tablespoons flaked coconut

Evenly arrange strawberries in piecrust. In a medium saucepan, combine dry gelatin, dry pudding mix, reserved pineapple liquid, and water. Cook over medium heat until mixture thickens and starts to boil, stirring often. Spoon hot sauce mixture evenly over strawberries. Refrigerate for at least 1 hour. In a medium bowl, combine drained pineapple and coconut extract. Add Cool Whip Lite. Mix gently to combine. Spread topping mixture evenly over set strawberry filling. Sprinkle coconut evenly over top. Refrigerate for at least 1 hour. Cut into 8 pieces.

Each serving equals:

DIABETIC EXCHANGES: 1 Starch • 1 Fat • ½ Fruit

187 Calories • 7 gm Fat • 2 gm Protein •
29 gm Carbohydrate • 251 mg Sodium • 2 gm Fiber

HE: 1 Bread • ½ Fruit • ¼ Slider •
19 Optional Calories

I get mail daily from people who've tried my Healthy Exchanges desserts. Here are just a few excerpts from their letters:

I'm the 70-year-old lady who wrote you a while back. I have lost the rest of my weight so I've lost 150 pounds in a year and a half and feel like I'm 30 again. I'm a retired nurse's aide living in Illinois and taking care of my aunt (81 and with Alzheimer's) and my uncle (74 and has emphysema). They love your pies! I make one every day. I have made 24 different pies and they are all delicious. Our favorites are Pineapple Fluff Pie and Tropical Fruit Pie. The whole neighborhood knows about your pies and nobody will believe they're diet pies. But I'm living proof. I ate a piece of every one of them and haven't gained a pound.

—M.H., IL

I wanted to let you know what a lifesaver your book has been for me. The recipes are so easy, and the desserts are incredible. When I tell people what I eat—the pies, the dessert salads—they look incredulous, but I've lost more than sixty pounds since February. And I've never felt so satisfied in my life!

—M.F., MI

I watched you on TV, then made the Triple Layer Party Pie. My husband loved it; we could both eat it and thoroughly enjoy it. I can now, at last, enjoy desserts also. Thank you, JoAnna, from the depths of my heart!

—C.M., OR

Your upbeat, positive attitude gives us hope that we can live a healthy lifestyle. I am a diabetic who has found new delights in your tasty and great-looking desserts. I have not let a week go by since meeting you without making at least two or three of them. So good, and so easy, too! Thank you for sharing your secrets of success.

—C.L., IN

When you spoke to our Mended Hearts support group, my blood sugar was 164, triglycerides were 946, and cholesterol was 268. After using your recipes for a few months, I had blood work done again. I'm delighted to report that my blood sugar was 80, triglycerides 181, and cholesterol 217. I have lost ten pounds, and the doctor was very happy with the report. He wants me to keep losing weight and stick with what I'm doing.

My husband has lost 16 pounds and says this is something we can both live with. We especially like the pies as they satisfy the sweet tooth.

—B.M., IA

Thank you for such a wonderful, helpful cookbook. I sent it to my sister and her husband. She has Type 2 diabetes and takes a pill each day, while her husband is insulin-dependent and injects himself twice a day. I sent the book to her and when she called, I told her to be sure to make the cherry pie filling. It was about 6 p.m. when she called me, groaning that she was full from her supper and how much she enjoyed the cherry pie! Her husband was so happy to have a delicious pie as he had craved a good slice of any kind. She couldn't believe how easy it was and with so few ingredients . . . Many thanks for such a good, easy-to-use cookbook with recipes to satisfy a hearty diabetic eater like my brother-in-law. He said that he always felt deprived and left out when it came to desserts, but not anymore!

—(8/97 NEWSLETTER)

When we had our Dessert Taste-Testing Buffet, one couple got up at 5 A.M. and drove seven hours from Nebraska in stormy weather to be there with us. The enthusiasm of all our guests meant a lot to Cliff and me, but that really touched my heart. Then there was the woman who came up to me after a cooking demo and simply said, "Your desserts are from heaven, and you are an angel!"

High praise, indeed. I do my best to earn it every day, and I hope you'll agree this book delivers everything I promise.

Jo Anna

Dessert
Every Night
by Rose Hoenig, R.D., L.D.

Dessert and diabetes. Do those words seem to clash? What else do you have to change now that you have diabetes? Suddenly, your thoughts are filled with taking medicine, weight management, physical activity, checking your blood glucose, doctor appointments and more. Did someone say "no more dessert?" No wonder desserts spelled backwards is STRESSED! Do you believe you have to give up all those mouthwatering favorites that come at the end of a meal or to celebrate a special occasion? There's got to be more for dessert besides a bowl of fruit!

Thanks to solid research showing that good blood glucose control can be achieved with the right balance of sugars and starches, desserts are no longer frowned upon. In fact, you might even see small amounts of regular sugars in some desserts planned for people with diabetes. With the release of the 1994 Nutrition Guidelines and Recommendations for Individuals with Diabetes by The American Diabetes Association, health care providers had scientific support to counsel their clients that they do not have to totally eliminate sugar. However, it continues to be important to consume a diet with the right amount of nutrients for you. Carbohydrates, fats, and proteins all contribute to the total calories in a food. It's often the fat content of a dessert that makes it so high in calories. All carbohydrates will raise blood glucose levels whether they come from grains, fruits, vegetables, or simple sugars. The total carbohydrate content of your meal plan balanced with the right amount of calories, physical activity, and medications, if needed, are the key to managing your diabetes. Preparing desserts with healthy ingredients is a consideration whether regular sugar, low-calorie sweeteners, or other foods contribute to its sweetness. Flavor is the primary reason we eat most foods, especially dessert. No one wants to sacrifice that just to make it low calorie. You can be confident that Healthy Exchange desserts will pass your taste test and desire for reduced carbohydrate and fat content. Your whole family can enjoy these foods and benefit from this without feeling deprived. Try them all and discover that you don't have to give up dessert or eat less tasty versions than everyone else!

How Do Desserts Fit Into a Diabetes Eating Plan?

The key to safely eating desserts as part of a healthy diet to control blood glucose is pretty simple. Remember to keep your portion to the one recommended on the recipe or label and allow for the carbohydrate and calories in your meal plan. Eating daily desserts without planning for the carbohydrate and calorie content can cause weight gain. Such foods are to be substituted for others in your meal plan, not just added because you know they are "diet." Diet doesn't always mean low calorie or low sugar. Even when it does, don't ignore the calories present. Eating more calories than your body needs for energy will cause you to store fat. For persons with Type I diabetes, the timing and amount of food eaten must be consistent. This can vary with the type of insulin that you use. In Type II diabetes, the focus of therapy is weight management to achieve near normal blood glucose and lipid or fat levels. So, you can see that you do need to pay attention to how much and when you eat.

Sugar is not a forbidden food. It is a simple carbohydrate as compared to starches, or complex carbohydrates, found in grains, vegetables, and legumes. You can substitute any carbohydrate choice for another of similar value in your meal. Simple sugars that provide equal amounts of carbohydrate are not found to raise blood glucose levels any more than starches. An example would be to substitute a dish of pudding for a piece of bread as long as the portion you use provides about the same amount of carbohydrate. That means you will probably need to prepare a reduced sugar pudding if you want a reasonable portion size. Foods sweetened with regular sugar usually exceed the carbohydrate of many other foods just because of the amount of sugar used in the product. Be cautious when using fat-free and sugar-free foods. They are not calorie free and do contain other forms of carbohydrate. Many fat-free and reduced-fat products are made with fat replacers that contain carbohydrate. Check the label if it is a prepared item or allow for this carbohydrate if you are preparing it yourself.

You may notice on the labels of some sugar-free foods that there are still calories present. This is due to the presence of sweetening ingredients known as sugar replacers or polyols. They are also known as sugar alcohols but do not contain any alcohol. On the label you will see them in the names of maltitol, mannitol, sorbitol, and xylitol. Polyols are a group of carbohydrates that are not sugars but still carbohydrates. They provide an average of 2 calories per gram compared to other carbohydrates at 4 calories per gram. Polyols are used to provide lower calorie sweetening and to add bulk or texture plus helping to retain moisture. They are like fiber in that they are incompletely absorbed and when eaten in large amounts can cause gastrointestinal upset. Polyols are slowly and incompletely absorbed, resulting in a lower blood glucose response. Do not use them to treat hypoglycemia or a low blood glucose as they will not raise blood glucose fast enough. The important thing to remember about using foods containing polyols is that they can contribute calories to your diet and if eaten in large amounts interfere with weight control and cause a laxative effect. The rule of thumb on how to count such foods is if the total carbohydrate is less than 10 grams, it is a free food. Likewise foods with less than 20 calories per serving are counted as free foods with a limit of three servings per day.

Do you have trouble with limiting portions of dessert? Out of sight, out of mind should be your motto! Whenever possible, cut all desserts into single serving portions and freeze what you can't eat. Pre-cut your pies and cover and put away all desserts after serving so you're not tempted to go back for more. Be sure you know just how many grams of carbohydrate are in a serving so you don't assume another serving really isn't going to add much to your meal.

The Exchange Lists for Meal Planning published by The American Diabetes and The American Dietetics Associations contain an "other carbohydrate" list of foods that can be interchanged with milk, fruit, and starch. You will often see in Healthy Exchange desserts and other recipes that the Diabetic Exchanges will include a starch/carbohydrate exchange. I have used this term to assist people in seeing that the recipe contains a mixture of carbohydrates that don't fit easily into just the starch group but contain enough carbohydrates to be counted.

Remember also, that many fat-free desserts do not contain significant amounts of nutrients so if eaten frequently they will replace other sources of vitamins, minerals and fiber. Here is an example of how Healthy Exchange desserts are good for you in ways besides being reduced in carbohydrate or fat. Many of these recipes contain unsweetened fruits, plain yogurt, and nonfat dry milk powder, which contribute to good nutrition.

Finally, it is important to self-monitor your blood glucose to be aware of how different foods affect your diabetes control. Fat-free foods can change the rate at which glucose is taken up into your blood. A food containing some fat will be more slowly absorbed than one without any fat. Many low-fat and fat-free products have ingredients added as bulking agents that can affect blood glucose levels in varying degrees because they are absorbed at different rates or barely absorbed at all. Even foods that have low-calorie sweeteners in them, such as diet desserts, will contain starches, other sugars, fats, and proteins. Because they contain a source of calories they will have some effect on your blood glucose. It is your responsibility to be aware of any significant effect on your diabetes control.

Beyond Dessert—
Eating for Good Health

In your pursuit to satisfy your sweet tooth, keep in mind that your ultimate goal is to manage your diabetes and achieve optimum good health. This is no different for you than for someone without diabetes except for the fact that having diabetes greatly increases your risk for cardiovascular related diseases including hypertension or high blood pressure and atherosclerosis that can cause heart attacks and strokes. Eating to manage diabetes should include low cholesterol and low saturated fat foods. The amount of fat that is right for you can be determined by your diabetes educator or dietitian. You may be advised to limit sodium in your diet. You can start by not using table salt on your food but also keep a close eye on the sodium in processed foods that you eat. Ask your physician or educator how much sodium is recommended when you are discussing your nutrition therapy. Finally, choose plenty of high-fiber foods and disease fighters containing antioxidants and phytochemicals such as whole grain cereals and breads, deep-colored fruits and vegetables, and foods like flax and soy. These foods contain substances found to help reduce cardiac risk and increase your immune system.

Eating is fun and eating delicious food is something we all look forward to. Don't feel left out because you have diabetes. Learn how to make your eating style work for you in managing your diabetes and helping you to feel good. Dessert can definitely be part of that plan.

Rose Hoenig, R.D., L.D., is a licensed, registered dietitian practicing in the Quad Cities. She is a graduate of Marycrest College and a member of the American Dietetic Association. She is also a member of the Iowa Consulting Dietitians in Health Care Facilities. Rose and her husband, Tony, live in Davenport, Iowa.

How to Read
a Healthy
Exchanges Recipe

The Healthy Exchanges Nutritional Analysis

Before using these recipes, you may wish to consult your physician or health-care provider to ensure that they are appropriate for you. The information in this book is not intended to take the place of any medical advice. It reflects my experiences, studies, research, and opinions regarding healthy eating.

Each recipe includes nutritional information calculated in three ways:

Healthy Exchanges Weight Loss Choices™ or Exchanges
Calories; Fat, Protein, Carbohydrates, and Fiber in grams;
    Sodium and Calcium in milligrams
Diabetic Exchanges

In every Healthy Exchanges recipe, the diabetic exchanges have been calculated by a registered dietitian. All the other calculations were done by computer, using the Food Processor II software. When the ingredient listing gives more than one choice, the first ingredient listed is the one used in the recipe analysis. Due to inevitable variations in the ingredients you choose to use, the nutritional values should be considered approximate.

Please note the following symbols:

☆ This star means that you should read the recipe's directions carefully for special instructions about **division** of ingredients.

✳ This symbol indicates **FREEZES WELL.**

Pudding Treats
and Salad Sweets

I came from a poor, working-class family, but my mother could make just about anything out of nothing. Because rice was so inexpensive, she made rice pudding for us all the time, but she rarely prepared it the same way twice. Whatever she had in the kitchen, she mixed into the bowl and surprised us. Our favorite versions were served warm, with raisins and cinnamon on top.

She also stirred up the wonderfully warm and soothing dessert that to this day feeds my soul like no other. Bread pudding required only those baking basics she had on hand—milk, eggs, sugar, and any kind of bread. That soft, sweet treat was then, and still is, the dish that makes me recall more than any other how much she loved me.

I think that's probably why I've created so many rice-pudding and bread-pudding recipes of my own. It goes back to my childhood and my memories of Mom's magic in the kitchen. Money was scarce during my growing-up years, but the food on the table was always abundant.

Now these sweet treats are easy to prepare and in much healthier versions: cool, creamy, smooth, and scrumptious rice puddings (*Chocolate Hawaiian Rice Pudding*). Warm, cozy bread puddings, fragrant with spices and the sweetness of fruit (*Black Forest Bread Pudding*). Tasty, light, and satisfying gelatin salads that tempt the palate with every spoonful (*Cranberry Fluff*). (We never had a family gathering that didn't include sweet salads along with the traditional ones!) Made with affection, garnished with love, they're sure to be welcomed by every member of the family!

These homey types of foods are coming back into style, as we remember those times when the world seemed smaller and safer.

They're high in flavor, and at the same time they're low in fat and sugar, and they feature small amounts of ingredients that are anything but diet food: chocolate graham crackers, pecans, flaked coconut, peanut butter, mini marshmallows, caramel sauce. For a light snack or the perfect ending to a big meal, I often think: *pudding or sweet salad.*

Butterscotch Pecan Parfait

Children always seem to love layered treats like this nutty one, so serving parfaits in clear dishes just increases the fun! My daughter, Becky, the butterscotch fan in the family, would be tempted by this for a homecoming celebration. ☻ Serves 6

¾ cup purchased graham cracker crumbs or 12 (2½-inch) graham cracker squares made into crumbs
¼ cup chopped pecans
1 (4-serving) package JELL-O sugar-free instant butterscotch pudding mix

⅔ cup Carnation Nonfat Dry Milk Powder
1½ cups water
¾ cup plain fat-free yogurt
1 teaspoon vanilla extract
10 tablespoons Cool Whip Lite ☆
3 maraschino cherries, halved

In a medium bowl, combine graham cracker crumbs and pecans. Set aside. In a large bowl, combine dry pudding mix and dry milk powder. Add water and yogurt. Mix well using a wire whisk. Blend in vanilla extract and ¼ cup Cool Whip Lite. Evenly spoon about ¼ cup pudding mixture into 6 dessert dishes. Sprinkle about 2 tablespoons graham cracker mixture evenly over each. Spoon about ¼ cup pudding mixture over graham cracker mixture. Sprinkle about 2 teaspoons graham cracker mixture over top of each, top with 1 tablespoon Cool Whip Lite, and garnish with cherry half. Refrigerate for at least 15 minutes.

Each serving equals:

DIABETIC EXCHANGES: 1 Starch/Carbohydrate • 1 Fat • ½ Fat Free Milk

141 Calories • 5 gm Fat • 5 gm Protein • 19 gm Carbohydrate • 334 mg Sodium • 150 mg Calcium • 0 gm Fiber

HE: ⅔ Bread • ⅔ Fat • ½ Fat Free Milk • ¼ Slider • 14 Optional Calories

Chocolate Pots de Creme Pudding

French restaurants are famous for piling on the calories and fat, but the food is so good, you're almost willing to throw caution and health concerns to the wind! You too can end your meal with a custard cup brimful of baked, rich creamy goodness—and no guilt. This version is sure to command a few "Ooh-la-las" at your house!

☻ Serves 4

> 1 (4-serving) package JELL-O sugar-free chocolate cook-and-serve
>   pudding mix
> ⅓ cup Carnation Nonfat Dry Milk Powder
> ½ cup water
> 1¼ cups black coffee
> 1 teaspoon brandy extract
> ¼ cup Cool Whip Lite

In a medium saucepan, combine dry pudding mix, dry milk powder, water, and coffee. Cook over medium heat until mixture thickens and starts to boil, stirring constantly. Remove from heat. Stir in brandy extract. Pour into 4 custard cups or dessert dishes. Refrigerate for at least 2 hours. Top each with 1 tablespoon Cool Whip Lite.

Each serving equals:

DIABETIC EXCHANGES: 1 Starch/Carbohydrate

56 Calories • 0 gm Fat • 3 gm Protein •
11 gm Carbohydrate • 142 mg Sodium •
70 mg Calcium • 0 gm Fiber

HE: ¼ Fat Free Milk • ¼ Slider •
15 Optional Calories

Almond Pudding Treats

My mother taught me so much about garnishing food beautifully, and this recipe is a perfect example. It's just a dish of almond pudding until I sprinkle those tasty slivered almonds over the top. Then—pudding with true pizzazz!   ● Serves 4

> 1 (4-serving) package JELL-O sugar-free instant vanilla pudding mix
> 2/3 cup Carnation Nonfat Dry Milk Powder
> 1 1/2 cups water
> 1/2 cup Cool Whip Free
> 1 teaspoon almond extract
> 1/4 cup slivered almonds ☆

In a large bowl, combine dry pudding mix, dry milk powder, and water. Mix well using a wire whisk. Blend in Cool Whip Free and almond extract. Add 3 tablespoons almonds. Mix gently to combine. Evenly spoon mixture into 4 dessert dishes. Sprinkle 3/4 teaspoon almonds over top of each. Refrigerate for at least 15 minutes.

Each serving equals:

DIABETIC EXCHANGES: 1 Starch/Carbohydrate •
1/2 Fat Free Milk • 1/2 Fat

---

128 Calories • 4 gm Fat • 6 gm Protein •
17 gm Carbohydrate • 392 mg Sodium •
160 mg Calcium • 1 gm Fiber

HE: 1/2 Fat Free Milk • 1/2 Fat • 1/4 Protein •
1/2 Slider

Sparkling Chocolate Pudding Treats

Just as champagne makes an evening sparkle and shine, this treasure chest of a dessert delivers shimmer and shine in every single bite! A marshmallow! A chocolate chip! A bit of coconut! Your pleasure is bound to bubble over!   ◐   Serves 4

> 1 (4-serving) package JELL-O sugar-free instant chocolate fudge
>   pudding mix
> ⅔ cup Carnation Nonfat Dry Milk Powder
> 1¼ cups water
> ½ cup Cool Whip Free ☆
> 1 teaspoon coconut extract
> ½ cup mini marshmallows
> 2 teaspoons flaked coconut
> 1 tablespoon mini chocolate chips

In a large bowl, combine dry pudding mix, dry milk powder, and water. Mix well using a wire whisk. Blend in ¼ cup Cool Whip Free and coconut extract. Add marshmallows. Mix gently to combine. Evenly spoon mixture into 4 dessert dishes. Top each with 1 tablespoon Cool Whip Free, ½ teaspoon coconut, and ¾ teaspoon chocolate chips.

Each serving equals:

DIABETIC EXCHANGES: 1 Starch/Carbohydrate •
½ Fat Free Milk

---

125 Calories • 1 gm Fat • 5 gm Protein •
24 gm Carbohydrate • 402 mg Sodium •
139 mg Calcium • 0 gm Fiber

HE: ½ Fat Free Milk • ¾ Slider • 9 Optional Calories

Mocha Mousse

If, when asked to choose your favorite flavor, you tend to waver between coffee and chocolate, this mousse is for you! Thick and rich, creamy and just a bit sophisticated, this scrumptious dessert is ideal for dinner parties, especially when the meal has been hearty. Everyone will find room for this lovely finale!　　◐　Serves 6

1 (8-ounce) package
   Philadelphia fat-free
   cream cheese
1½ cups plain fat-free yogurt
⅓ cup Carnation Nonfat Dry
   Milk Powder
2 tablespoons Splenda
   Granular
1 teaspoon vanilla extract

¾ cup water
1 (4-serving) package JELL-O
   sugar-free instant
   chocolate fudge
   pudding mix
1 teaspoon instant coffee
   crystals
¾ cup Cool Whip Free

In a large bowl, stir cream cheese with a spoon until soft. Add yogurt and dry milk powder. Mix well to combine. Stir in Splenda, vanilla extract, and water. Add dry pudding mix and instant coffee powder. Mix well using a wire whisk. Fold in Cool Whip Free. Evenly spoon mixture into 6 dessert dishes. Refrigerate for at least 30 minutes.

Each serving equals:

DIABETIC EXCHANGES: 1 Meat • ½ Fat Free Milk •
½ Starch/Carbohydrate *or* 1 Meat •
1 Starch/Carbohydrate

112 Calories • 0 gm Fat • 11 gm Protein •
17 gm Carbohydrate • 515 mg Sodium •
159 mg Calcium • 0 gm Fiber

HE: ⅔ Protein • ½ Fat Free Milk • ¼ Slider •
17 Optional Calories

Cheesecake Pudding

Ever have a day when you just yearned for cheesecake, but there wasn't a piecrust in the house? It's happened to me, and this was my smart and satisfying solution! You may be astonished at how much like the real thing this easy dessert tastes!   ☻   Serves 4

1 (8-ounce) package
   Philadelphia fat-free
   cream cheese
1 (4-serving) package JELL-O
   sugar-free instant vanilla
   pudding mix
⅔ cup Carnation Nonfat Dry
   Milk Powder
1⅓ cups water

2 teaspoons lemon juice
1 tablespoon Splenda Granular
1 teaspoon vanilla extract
3 tablespoons purchased
   graham cracker crumbs
   or 3 (2½-inch) graham
   cracker squares made
   into crumbs
¼ cup Cool Whip Lite

In a medium bowl, stir cream cheese with a spoon until soft. Add dry pudding mix, dry milk powder, and water. Mix well using a wire whisk. Stir in lemon juice, Splenda, and vanilla extract. Spoon mixture evenly into 4 parfait glasses. Refrigerate for at least 1 hour. When serving, sprinkle each with about ¾ tablespoon graham cracker crumbs and top with 1 tablespoon Cool Whip Lite.

Each serving equals:

DIABETIC EXCHANGES: 1 Meat • ½ Fat Free Milk •
½ Starch/Carbohydrate *or* 1 Meat •
1 Starch/Carbohydrate

133 Calories • 1 gm Fat • 12 gm Protein •
19 gm Carbohydrate • 773 mg Sodium •
138 mg Calcium • 0 mg Fiber

HE: 1 Protein • ½ Fat Free Milk • ¼ Bread •
¼ Slider • 17 Optional Calories

Imperial White Chocolate Parfait

Here's something worth riding over the snow-covered Russian steppes to taste! When the last emperor was in power, this beautiful dessert might have been deemed worthy to be served at his banquet table, don't you think?   ☻   Serves 4

1 (4-serving) package JELL-O
   sugar-free instant white
   chocolate pudding mix
⅔ cup Carnation Nonfat Dry
   Milk Powder
1½ cups water
½ cup Cool Whip Free

1 teaspoon coconut extract
2 cups (2 medium) diced
   bananas
1 tablespoon mini chocolate
   chips
1 tablespoon flaked coconut

In a medium bowl, combine dry pudding mix, dry milk powder, and water. Mix well using a wire whisk. Blend in Cool Whip Free and coconut extract. Add bananas. Mix gently to combine. Evenly spoon mixture into 4 parfait or dessert dishes. Top each with ¾ teaspoon chocolate chips and coconut. Refrigerate for at least 30 minutes.

HINT: To prevent bananas from turning brown, mix with 1 teaspoon lemon juice or sprinkle with Fruit Fresh.

Each serving equals:

DIABETIC EXCHANGES: 1 Fruit • 1 Starch/Carbohydrate
• ½ Fat Free Milk

---

165 Calories • 1 gm Fat • 4 gm Protein •
35 gm Carbohydrate • 401 mg Sodium •
143 mg Calcium • 2 gm Fiber

HE: 1 Fruit • ½ Fat Free Milk • ¾ Slider •
13 Optional Calories

Banana Peanut Butter Delights

Remember peanut butter and banana sandwiches when you were a kid? Well, even if you never feasted on that childhood favorite, take it from me—this is a winning combination! It's easy to fix, and tastes wonderfully old-fashioned, too.   ☻   Serves 4

> 1 (4-serving) package JELL-O sugar-free instant banana cream pudding mix
> ⅔ cup Carnation Nonfat Dry Milk Powder
> 1½ cups water
> 2 tablespoons Peter Pan reduced-fat peanut butter
> ½ cup Cool Whip Lite ☆
> ¼ cup chopped dry-roasted peanuts ☆
> 2 cups (2 medium) diced bananas

In a large bowl, combine dry pudding mix, dry milk powder, and water. Mix well using a wire whisk. Blend in peanut butter and ¼ cup Cool Whip Lite. Reserve 2 teaspoons peanuts for garnish. Gently stir in remaining peanuts and bananas. Evenly spoon mixture into 4 dessert dishes. Top each with 1 tablespoon Cool Whip Lite and ½ teaspoon peanuts. Refrigerate for at least 15 minutes.

Each serving equals:

DIABETIC EXCHANGES: 1 Fruit • 1 Fat •
1 Starch/Carbohydrate • ½ Fat Free Milk

256 Calories • 8 gm Fat • 9 gm Protein •
37 gm Carbohydrate • 440 mg Sodium •
147 mg Calcium • 3 gm Fiber

HE: 1 Fruit • 1 Fat • ¾ Protein • ½ Fat Free Milk
• ½ Slider • 5 Optional Calories

Tropical Isle Custards

I have a whole little shelf in my cupboard just filled with bottles of extracts, and you'll see that I like to stir them into many of my desserts. Just a tiny amount delivers so much flavor, as it does in this sunny, fruity recipe that will send tropical breezes blowing through your kitchen all year round! ☯ Serves 4

1 (11-ounce) can mandarin oranges, rinsed and drained

1 (4-serving) package JELL-O sugar-free vanilla cook-and-serve pudding mix

⅔ cup Carnation Nonfat Dry Milk Powder

1 (8-ounce) can crushed pineapple, packed in fruit juice, undrained

1 cup water

1 teaspoon coconut extract

1 tablespoon + 1 teaspoon flaked coconut

1 tablespoon chopped pecans

Evenly divide mandarin oranges among four (1-cup) custard dishes. In a medium saucepan, combine dry pudding mix, dry milk powder, undrained pineapple, and water. Cook over medium heat until mixture thickens and starts to boil, stirring often. Remove from heat. Stir in coconut extract. Evenly spoon hot mixture over mandarin oranges. Refrigerate for at least 30 minutes. Just before serving, sprinkle 1 teaspoon coconut and ¾ teaspoon pecans over top of each.

Each serving equals:

DIABETIC EXCHANGES: 1 Fruit • ½ Fat Free Milk • ½ Fat • ½ Starch/Carbohydrate *or* 1 Fruit • 1 Starch/Carbohydrate • ½ Fat

154 Calories • 2 gm Fat • 5 gm Protein • 29 gm Carbohydrate • 185 mg Sodium • 156 mg Calcium • 1 gm Fiber

HE: 1 Fruit • ½ Fat Free Milk • ¼ Fat • ¼ Slider • 5 Optional Calories

Coconut Berry Creams

If you're looking for something spectacular to serve at a summer cookout, or you've just been blueberry picking and have tons of the luscious purple-blue gems on hand, this is a lovely recipe to try! It's also pretty enough to serve to your company at a festive bridal shower. ❂ Serves 4

> 1 (4-serving) package JELL-O sugar-free instant vanilla
>   pudding mix
> ⅔ cup Carnation Nonfat Dry Milk Powder
> 1 cup Diet Mountain Dew
> 1 teaspoon coconut extract
> ¾ cup plain fat-free yogurt
> ½ cup Cool Whip Free
> 1½ cups fresh blueberries
> 1 tablespoon + 1 teaspoon flaked coconut

In a large bowl, combine dry pudding mix, dry milk powder, and Diet Mountain Dew. Mix well using a wire whisk. Blend in coconut extract, yogurt, and Cool Whip Free. Gently stir in blueberries. Evenly spoon mixture into 4 dessert dishes. Sprinkle 1 teaspoon coconut over top of each. Refrigerate for at least 15 minutes.

Each serving equals:

DIABETIC EXCHANGES: ½ Fat Free Milk • ½ Fruit •
½ Starch/Carbohydrate *or* 1 Skim Milk •
1 Starch/Carbohydrate

146 Calories • 2 gm Fat • 7 gm Protein •
25 gm Carbohydrate • 437 mg Sodium •
226 mg Calcium • 2 mg Fiber

HE: ¾ Fat Free Milk • ½ Fruit • ½ Slider •
5 Optional Calories

French Chocolate Orange Mousse

There's something so *délicieux* about the blend of orange and choco-late, it's one of the most popular dessert combos both here and abroad! This dish also packs a great healthy wallop of calcium in every serving, so enjoy it—it's good for you! ☻ Serves 4

1 (4-serving) package sugar-free instant chocolate fudge
     pudding mix
⅔ cup Carnation Nonfat Dry Milk Powder
1 cup unsweetened orange juice
¾ cup plain fat-free yogurt
½ cup Cool Whip Free
1 (11-ounce) can mandarin oranges, rinsed and drained ☆
3 (2½-inch) chocolate graham crackers made into fine crumbs

In a large bowl, combine dry pudding mix, dry milk powder, and orange juice. Mix well using a wire whisk. Blend in yogurt and Cool Whip Free. Reserve 4 mandarin oranges. Gently stir remaining mandarin oranges into pudding mixture. Evenly spoon mixture into 4 dessert dishes. Sprinkle graham cracker crumbs evenly over tops and garnish each with a reserved mandarin orange. Refrigerate for at least 30 minutes.

Each serving equals:

DIABETIC EXCHANGES: 1 Fat Free Milk • 1 Fruit •
½ Starch/Carbohydrate

---

172 Calories • 0 gm Fat • 8 gm Protein •
35 mg Carbohydrate • 450 mg Sodium •
235 mg Calcium • 0 gm Fiber

HE: 1 Fruit • ¾ Fat Free Milk • ¼ Bread •
½ Slider • 10 Optional Calories

Dried Fruit Tapioca Pudding

Cliff is a big fan of tapioca, so I use my imagination to create puddings to please him in particular. (I'm no fool!) This is a simple way to add flavor and interest to a classic, even if you've only got a bit of dried fruit in your pantry. ☺ Serves 4

> 2 cups fat-free milk
> 1 (4-serving) package JELL-O sugar-free vanilla cook-and-serve pudding mix
> 2 tablespoons quick tapioca
> ¼ cup raisins
> ¼ cup chopped dried apricots
> 1 teaspoon vanilla extract
> ¼ cup Cool Whip Lite
> Dash ground cinnamon

In a medium saucepan, combine milk, dry pudding mix, tapioca, raisins, and chopped apricots. Let set for 5 minutes. Cook over medium heat until mixture thickens and starts to boil, stirring constantly. Remove from heat. Stir in vanilla extract. Evenly spoon mixture into 4 dessert dishes. Refrigerate for at least 2 hours. When serving, top each with 1 tablespoon Cool Whip Lite and lightly sprinkle with cinnamon.

Each serving equals:

DIABETIC EXCHANGES: 1 Fruit •
½ Starch/Carbohydrate • ½ Fat Free Milk *or* 1 Fruit •
1 Starch/Carbohydrate

---

132 Calories • 0 gm Fat • 5 gm Protein •
28 gm Carbohydrate • 180 mg Sodium •
160 mg Calcium • 1 gm Fiber

HE: 1 Fruit • ½ Fat Free Milk • ½ Slider •
5 Optional Calories

New "Old-Fashioned" Rice Pudding

Cliff, my husband, business partner, and Official Taste Tester, kept hanging around the kitchen the week I was testing the rice pudding recipes. He knew, as I do, that nothing is more soothing after a busy day than rice pudding—especially served up the old-time way, with raisins and cinnamon! ☉ Serves 6

> 4 cups fat-free milk
> 1 (4-serving) package JELL-O sugar-free vanilla cook-and-serve
>   pudding mix
> 1 cup uncooked Minute Rice
> ½ cup raisins
> ½ teaspoon ground cinnamon

In a large saucepan, combine milk, dry pudding mix, uncooked rice, and raisins. Cook over medium heat until mixture thickens and starts to boil, stirring constantly. Remove from heat. Place saucepan on a wire rack. Stir in cinnamon. Cover and let set for 5 minutes. Stir again. Evenly spoon mixture into 6 dessert dishes. Refrigerate for at least 30 minutes.

Each serving equals:

DIABETIC EXCHANGES: 1 Fruit • 1 Fat Free Milk

132 Calories • 0 gm Fat • 6 gm Protein •
27 gm Carbohydrate • 163 mg Sodium •
211 mg Calcium • 1 gm Fiber

HE: ⅔ Fruit • ⅔ Fat Free Milk • ½ Bread •
13 Optional Calories

Rice Peach Melba Pudding

If you've never enjoyed the delightful dessert known as Peach Melba, here are two hints about why it's so beloved: raspberries and peaches! *Mmm*—doesn't that sound scrumptious when combined with creamy rice pudding? ◐ Serves 6

> 1 (4-serving) package JELL-O sugar-free vanilla cook-and-
>   serve pudding mix
> 2 cups fat-free milk
> 1 teaspoon vanilla extract
> 1⅓ cups uncooked Minute Rice
> 1 (16-ounce) can peaches, packed in fruit juice,
>   drained, and coarsely chopped, and ¼ cup liquid
>   reserved
> 1 (4-serving) package JELL-O sugar-free raspberry
>   gelatin
> 1 tablespoon cornstarch
> ¼ cup water
> 1½ cups fresh raspberries
> 6 tablespoons Cool Whip Lite

In a medium saucepan, combine dry pudding mix and milk. Cook over medium heat until mixture thickens and starts to boil, stirring constantly. Remove from heat. Stir in vanilla extract, uncooked rice, and chopped peaches. Place saucepan on a wire rack, cover, and let set. Meanwhile, in a small saucepan, combine dry gelatin and cornstarch. Add reserved peach liquid and water. Mix well to combine. Cook over medium heat until mixture thickens and starts to boil, stirring constantly. Remove from heat. Gently stir in raspberries. Place saucepan on a wire rack and allow to cool for 15 minutes. Gently fold raspberry mixture into rice mixture. Evenly spoon mixture into 6 dessert dishes. Refrigerate for at least 30 minutes. When serving, top each with 1 tablespoon Cool Whip Lite.

Each serving equals:

DIABETIC EXCHANGES: 1 Fruit • 1 Starch/Carbohydrate

144 Calories • 0 gm Fat • 5 gm Protein •
31 gm Carbohydrate • 159 mg Sodium •
115 mg Calcium • 3 gm Fiber

HE: 1 Fruit • ⅔ Bread • ⅓ Fat Free Milk •
¼ Slider • 15 Optional Calories

Chocolate Hawaiian Rice Pudding

I doubt if rice pudding is truly an island tradition, but imagine how those first missionaries might have been welcomed to Hawaii if they'd only offered the locals a dish of this festive blend! Every bite is a fresh surprise, with tasty fruit and nuts to win you over. When you want your guests to feel welcome, say "Aloha!" with this.

☺ Serves 6

> 1 (4-serving) package JELL-O sugar-free chocolate cook-and-serve pudding mix
> ⅔ cup Carnation Nonfat Dry Milk Powder
> 1 (8-ounce) can crushed pineapple, packed in fruit juice, undrained
> 1¼ cups water
> 1 teaspoon coconut extract
> 1½ cups cold, cooked rice
> ¾ cup Cool Whip Free
> 2 tablespoons chopped pecans
> 2 tablespoons flaked coconut
> 3 maraschino cherries, halved

In a large saucepan, combine dry pudding mix, dry milk powder, undrained pineapple, and water. Cook over medium heat until mixture thickens and starts to boil, stirring often. Remove from heat. Add coconut extract and rice. Mix well to combine. Place saucepan on a wire rack and allow to cool for 30 minutes. Stir in Cool Whip Free and pecans. Evenly spoon mixture into 6 dessert dishes. Top each with 1 teaspoon coconut and maraschino cherry half. Serve at once or refrigerate until ready to serve.

HINT: 1 cup uncooked instant rice usually cooks to about 1½ cups.

Each serving equals:

DIABETIC EXCHANGES: 2 Starch/Carbohydrate

154 Calories • 2 gm Fat • 4 gm Protein •
30 gm Carbohydrate • 125 mg Sodium •
102 mg Calcium • 1 gm Fiber

HE: ½ Bread • ⅓ Fruit • ⅓ Fat • ⅓ Fat Free Milk •
½ Slider

Bread Pudding with Pecan Sauce

It's amazing how little of an ingredient it takes to please your heart and excite your taste buds! For me, just a spoonful or so of pecans is enough to make me feel like the dish before me is a special treat, so this pudding dish makes an ordinary day a reason for celebrating.

☻ Serves 6

2 (4-serving) packages JELL-O sugar-free vanilla cook-and-serve pudding mix ☆
⅔ cup Carnation Nonfat Dry Milk Powder
3¼ cups water ☆
2 teaspoons ground cinnamon ☆
2 teaspoons vanilla extract ☆
½ cup raisins
8 slices reduced-calorie white bread, torn into pieces
2 tablespoons chopped pecans
2 teaspoons I Can't Believe It's Not Butter! Light Margarine

Preheat oven to 350 degrees. Spray an 8-by-8-inch baking dish with butter-flavored cooking spray. In a large bowl, combine 1 package dry pudding mix, dry milk powder, and 1¾ cups water. Mix well using a wire whisk. Blend in 1 teaspoon cinnamon, 1 teaspoon vanilla extract, and raisins. Add bread pieces. Mix well to combine. Pour mixture into prepared baking dish. Bake for 45 to 50 minutes. Place baking dish on a wire rack and allow to cool for 15 minutes. Cover and refrigerate for at least 1 hour. Just before serving, in a medium saucepan, combine remaining package dry pudding mix and remaining 1½ cups water. Stir in remaining 1 teaspoon cinnamon and pecans. Cook over medium heat until mixture thickens and starts to boil, stirring constantly. Remove from heat. Stir in remaining 1 teaspoon vanilla extract and margarine. Cut bread pudding into 6 servings. For each serving, place 1 piece of bread pudding on dessert plate and spoon about ¼ cup hot pecan sauce over top.

Each serving equals:

DIABETIC EXCHANGES: 1 Starch/Carbohydrate •
1 Fruit • ½ Fat

---

174 Calories • 2 gm Fat • 6 gm Protein •
33 gm Carbohydrate • 356 mg Sodium •
131 mg Calcium • 4 gm Fiber

HE: ⅔ Bread • ⅔ Fruit • ½ Fat • ⅓ Fat Free Milk •
¼ Slider • 7 Optional Calories

Old-Fashioned Bread Pudding

One of my favorite challenges in Healthy Exchanges is making foods taste as warm and cozy as we remember them, but still easy to prepare and healthy, too! Bread pudding is a comfort food classic that recalls the sweetest childhood memories for me. Why not start a new tradition in your family with this wonderful version?

● Serves 6

1 (4-serving) package JELL-O
    sugar-free vanilla cook-
    and-serve pudding mix
¼ cup Splenda Granular ☆
2 (12-fluid-ounce) cans
    Carnation Evaporated
    Fat Free Milk

½ cup raisins
1 teaspoon vanilla extract
1 tablespoon I Can't Believe It's
    Not Butter! Light Margarine
6 slices reduced-calorie white
    bread, torn into pieces
½ teaspoon apple pie spice

Preheat oven to 350 degrees. Spray an 8-by-8-inch baking dish with butter-flavored cooking spray. In a large saucepan, combine dry pudding mix, 2 tablespoons Splenda, and evaporated fat-free milk. Add raisins. Mix well to combine. Cook over medium heat until mixture thickens and starts to boil, stirring constantly. Remove from heat. Stir in vanilla extract and margarine. Add bread pieces. Mix gently to combine. Pour mixture into prepared baking dish. In a small bowl, combine remaining 2 tablespoons Splenda and apple pie spice. Evenly sprinkle mixture over top. Bake for 15 minutes. Cut into 6 servings. Serve warm or cold.

Each serving equals:

DIABETIC EXCHANGES: 1 Fat Free Milk • 1 Fruit •
½ Starch/Carbohydrate

201 Calories • 1 gm Fat • 12 gm Protein •
36 gm Carbohydrate • 349 mg Sodium •
393 mg Calcium • 3 gm Fiber

HE: 1 Fat Free Milk • ⅔ Fruit • ½ Bread • ¼ Fat •
17 Optional Calories

Black Forest Bread Pudding

Talk about luscious and irresistible—and you'd probably be cheering this oh-so-tasty concoction! Instead of the usual creamy custard, I've stirred up some chocolate fireworks, with cherries the crowning glory. This one is party food you can enjoy anytime!

● Serves 4 (1 cup)

> 1 (4-serving) package JELL-O sugar-free chocolate cook-and-serve pudding mix
> ⅔ cup Carnation Nonfat Dry Milk Powder
> 1 (16-ounce) can tart red cherries, packed in water, drained, and ½ cup liquid reserved
> 1½ cups water
> ½ teaspoon almond extract
> 6 slices reduced-calorie white bread, torn into pieces
> 2 tablespoons slivered almonds

Preheat oven to 350 degrees. Spray four (1-cup) custard cups with butter-flavored cooking spray. In a large saucepan, combine dry pudding mix, dry milk powder, reserved cherry liquid, and water. Cook over medium heat until mixture thickens and starts to boil, stirring constantly. Remove from heat. Stir in almond extract. Add cherries and bread pieces. Mix gently to combine. Spread mixture into prepared custard cups. Evenly sprinkle almonds over top. Place custard cups on a baking sheet and bake for 30 minutes. Good warm or cold.

Each serving equals:

DIABETIC EXCHANGES: 1 Fruit •
1 Starch/Carbohydrate • ½ Fat Free Milk • ½ Fat

219 Calories • 3 gm Fat • 10 gm Protein •
38 gm Carbohydrate • 353 mg Sodium •
188 mg Calcium • 5 gm Fiber

HE: 1 Fruit • ¾ Bread • ½ Fat Free Milk • ¼ Fat •
¼ Slider • 12 Optional Calories

Tropical Paradise Gelatin Salad

This layered salad is a perfect party dish, refreshing and colorful, and wonderfully tasty. Even if the nearest you'll get this year to the Caribbean is watching a hurricane's progress on the Weather Channel, you deserve a taste of paradise to warm your heart *and* your soul!   ◐   Serves 8

> 2 (4-serving) packages JELL-O sugar-free strawberry-kiwi
>   gelatin
> 1¼ cups boiling water
> 1¼ cups cold water
> 1 (8-ounce) can pineapple tidbits, packed in fruit juice, drained,
>   and ¼ cup liquid reserved
> 2 cups sliced fresh strawberries
> 1 cup (1 medium) sliced banana
> 1 cup Cool Whip Free
> ¼ cup Land O Lakes no-fat sour cream
> 1 teaspoon coconut extract
> 1 (8-ounce) can crushed pineapple, packed in fruit juice, drained
> 2 tablespoons flaked coconut

In a large bowl, combine dry gelatin and boiling water. Mix well to dissolve gelatin. Stir in cold water and reserved pineapple liquid. Add pineapple tidbits, strawberries, and banana. Mix well to combine. Pour mixture into an 8-by-12-inch dish. Refrigerate until firm, about 3 hours. In a large bowl, combine Cool Whip Free and sour cream. Add coconut extract and crushed pineapple. Mix gently to combine. Spread mixture evenly over set gelatin. Evenly sprinkle coconut over top. Refrigerate for at least 30 minutes. Cut into 8 servings.

HINTS: 1. If you can't find pineapple tidbits, use chunk pineapple
           and coarsely chop.
       2. To prevent banana from turning brown, mix with 1 tea-
           spoon lemon juice or sprinkle with Fruit Fresh.

Each serving equals:

DIABETIC EXCHANGES: 1 Fruit • ½ Starch/Carbohydrate

100 Calories • 0 gm Fat • 2 gm Protein •
23 gm Carbohydrate • 73 mg Sodium •
23 mg Calcium • 1 gm Fiber

HE: 1 Fruit • ¼ Slider • 11 Optional Calories

Layered Pear Gelatin Salad

Layered salads take more time to prepare, but the "oohs" and "ahhs" can definitely be worth it! This looks lovely on the plate, but it tastes even better when you and your family gobble it down. If you're feeling adventurous, you could try this dish with fruit cocktail sometime!　❤　Serves 8

1 (4-serving) package JELL-O
　　sugar-free lime gelatin
1 cup boiling water
1 (16-ounce) can pears, packed
　　in fruit juice, drained,
　　and ½ cup liquid reserved
¼ cup water

1 (8-ounce) package
　　Philadelphia fat-free
　　cream cheese
1 tablespoon lemon juice
1 cup Cool Whip Lite
3 to 4 drops green food coloring

In a large bowl, combine dry gelatin and boiling water. Mix well to dissolve gelatin. Add reserved pear liquid and water to gelatin mixture. Mix well to combine. Reserve ½ cup of gelatin mixture at room temperature. Pour remaining gelatin mixture into an 8-by-8-inch dish. Refrigerate until set, about 1 hour. In a medium bowl, stir cream cheese with a spoon until soft. Add lemon juice and room-temperature gelatin. Mix well to combine. Coarsely chop pears and fold into cream cheese mixture. Spread mixture evenly over set gelatin. Refrigerate for 1 hour. In a small bowl, combine Cool Whip Lite and green food coloring. Evenly spread mixture over cream cheese mixture. Refrigerate for at least 2 hours. Cut into 8 servings.

Each serving equals:

DIABETIC EXCHANGES: ½ Fruit • ½ Meat •
½ Starch/Carbohydrate

81 Calories • 1 gm Fat • 5 gm Protein •
13 gm Carbohydrate • 201 mg Sodium •
3 mg Calcium • 1 gm Fiber

HE: ½ Fruit • ½ Protein • ¼ Slider •
5 Optional Calories

Sunny Isle Apple Salad

Every rainbow promises a pot of gold at the end, and I like providing my own little bit of mealtime treasure: a salad inspired by the Golden Delicious apple. Coupled with celery, nuts, and pineapple, it's enough to make the sun shine on the cloudiest day of the year!

● Serves 6 (¾ cup)

> ½ cup Cool Whip Free
> 1 teaspoon coconut extract
> 2 cups (4 small) cored, unpeeled, and chopped Golden Delicious
>   apples
> ¾ cup finely chopped celery
> 1 (8-ounce) can pineapple chunks, packed in fruit juice, drained
> ¼ cup chopped pecans
> 2 tablespoons flaked coconut

In a medium bowl, combine Cool Whip Free and coconut extract. Add apples, celery, pineapple, and pecans. Mix gently to combine. Cover and refrigerate for at least 15 minutes. When serving, sprinkle 1 teaspoon coconut over each serving.

Each serving equals:

DIABETIC EXCHANGES: 1 Fruit • 1 Fat

100 Calories • 4 gm Fat • 0 gm Protein • 16 gm Carbohydrate • 21 mg Sodium • 16 mg Calcium • 2 gm Fiber

HE: 1 Fruit • ⅔ Fat • ¼ Vegetable • 15 Optional Calories

Apple Crumb Salad

I always cheer the arrival of fall, because the Red Delicious apples are never shinier or more gorgeously red! This crunchy-sweet combo tastes old-fashioned and makes a terrific side dish with a pork entree.   ☽   Serves 6 (¾ cup)

> 1 (4-serving) package JELL-O sugar-free instant vanilla pudding
>   mix
> ⅔ cup Carnation Nonfat Dry Milk Powder
> 1 cup unsweetened apple juice
> ¾ cup plain fat-free yogurt
> ½ cup Cool Whip Free
> 1 teaspoon vanilla extract
> ½ teaspoon apple pie spice
> 2 cups (4 small) cored, unpeeled, and diced Red Delicious apples
> 3 tablespoons chopped pecans
> 9 (2½-inch) graham cracker squares made into large crumbs

In a large bowl, combine dry pudding mix and dry milk powder. Add apple juice. Mix well using a wire whisk. Blend in yogurt, Cool Whip Free, vanilla extract, and apple pie spice. Add apples, pecans, and graham cracker crumbs. Mix gently to combine. Cover and refrigerate for at least 15 minutes. Gently stir again just before serving.

Each serving equals:

DIABETIC EXCHANGES: 1 Fruit • 1 Starch/Carbohydrate • ½ Fat

---

155 Calories • 3 gm Fat • 5 gm Protein • 27 gm Carbohydrate • 321 mg Sodium • 155 mg Calcium • 1 gm Fiber

---

HE: 1 Fruit • ½ Fat • ½ Bread • ½ Fat Free Milk • ¼ Slider • 6 Optional Calories

Peanut Butter Fruit Salad

If you've always wanted a tasty dressing to pour over fresh fruit, I think you'll be delighted after you try this dazzling concoction! It's a little bit nutty, a little bit creamy, a little bit fruity, and a whole lot yummy!　❍　Serves 4

> 1 cup (1 medium) sliced banana
> 1 (8-ounce) can pineapple tidbits, packed in fruit juice, drained,
> 　　and ¼ cup liquid reserved
> ⅓ cup Carnation Nonfat Dry Milk Powder
> ½ cup water
> ¼ cup Peter Pan reduced-fat peanut butter
> ½ teaspoon coconut extract
> 2 teaspoons flaked coconut

In a medium bowl, combine banana and pineapple. In a small bowl, combine dry milk powder, reserved pineapple liquid, and water. Blend in peanut butter and coconut extract. Mix well until smooth. Evenly spoon fruit into 4 dessert dishes. Spoon about 2 tablespoons peanut butter mixture over fruit and garnish each with ½ teaspoon coconut. Refrigerate for at least 15 minutes.

HINTS: 1. To prevent banana from turning brown, mix with 1 teaspoon lemon juice or sprinkle with Fruit Fresh.
2. If you can't find tidbits, use chunk pineapple and coarsely chop.

Each serving equals:

DIABETIC EXCHANGES: 1 Fruit • 1 Starch/Carbohydrate • 1 Fat • ½ Meat

198 Calories • 6 gm Fat • 7 gm Protein • 29 gm Carbohydrate • 109 mg Sodium • 80 mg Calcium • 2 gm Fiber

HE: 1 Fruit • 1 Fat • 1 Protein • ¼ Fat Free Milk • 2 Optional Calories

Fluffy Fruit Cocktail Salad

Everyone needs calcium to build and maintain strong, healthy bones, but if you're having trouble downing the milk you should try putting dishes like this one on your family's menu! Each serving provides nearly a cup of skim milk, but what you taste is just rich and creamy goodness. ☻ Serves 6 (¾ cup)

1 cup Carnation Nonfat Dry
    Milk Powder ☆
1 cup water
2 teaspoons white vinegar
¾ cup plain fat-free yogurt
1 teaspoon vanilla extract
2 tablespoons Splenda Granular
¾ cup Cool Whip Free
1 (4-serving) package JELL-O
    sugar-free instant vanilla
    pudding mix

1 (16-ounce) can fruit cocktail,
    packed in fruit juice,
    drained
1 (11-ounce) can mandarin
    oranges, rinsed and
    drained
½ cup mini marshmallows

In a small bowl, combine ⅔ cup dry milk powder, water, and vinegar. Let set. Meanwhile in another small bowl, combine yogurt and remaining ⅓ cup dry milk powder. Stir in vanilla extract and Splenda. Add Cool Whip Free. Mix gently to combine. In a large bowl, combine dry pudding mix and milk mixture. Mix well using a wire whisk. Blend in yogurt mixture. Add fruit cocktail, mandarin oranges, and marshmallows. Mix gently to combine. Cover and refrigerate for at least 30 minutes. Gently stir again just before serving.

Each serving equals:

DIABETIC EXCHANGES: 1 Fruit • 1 Starch/Carbohydrate

156 Calories • 0 gm Fat • 6 gm Protein •
33 gm Carbohydrate • 316 mg Sodium •
207 mg Calcium • 1 gm Fiber

HE: 1 Fruit • ⅔ Fat Free Milk • ¼ Slider •
17 Optional Calories

Hawaiian Moonlight Salad

Is it just my imagination, or does the moon look bigger when you're walking on a tropical beach? Maybe it's because there seems to be so much sky over the ocean! Even if a trip to Waikiki is out of the question, treat yourself to this mouthwatering salad that brims with the flavors of those lovely islands! ☾ Serves 8

2 (4-serving) packages
    JELLO sugar-free lime
    gelatin
2 cups boiling water
2 (8-ounce) cans crushed
    pineapple, packed in
    fruit juice, undrained
3/4 cup plain fat-free yogurt

1/3 cup Carnation Nonfat Dry
    Milk Powder
2 tablespoons Splenda
    Granular
1 teaspoon coconut extract
1/4 cup chopped pecans
3/4 cup Cool Whip Lite
2 tablespoons flaked coconut

In a large bowl, combine dry gelatin and boiling water. Mix well to dissolve gelatin. Stir in undrained pineapple. In a small bowl, combine yogurt, dry milk powder, Splenda, and coconut extract. Add to gelatin mixture. Mix well until smooth. Stir in pecans. Pour into an 8-by-8-inch dish. Refrigerate until set, about 2 hours. Spread Cool Whip Lite evenly over set gelatin and sprinkle coconut over top. Cut into 8 servings.

Each serving equals:

DIABETIC EXCHANGES: 1 Fat • 1/2 Fruit •
1/2 Starch/Carbohydrate

116 Calories • 4 gm Fat • 4 gm Protein •
16 gm Carbohydrate • 89 mg Sodium •
87 mg Calcium • 1 gm Fiber

HE: 1/2 Fruit • 1/2 Fat • 1/4 Fat Free Milk •
1/4 Slider • 10 Optional Calories

Mandarin Tapioca Salad

"Simply splendid" is how a restaurant reviewer might describe this dish that has so much flavor it might leave you breathless! Orange times three plus the old-timey goodness of tapioca make it a treat for all occasions. And if you've never tried tapioca, here's a great way to make its acquaintance. ☻ Serves 6 (⅔ cup)

1 (4-serving) package JELL-O
    sugar-free vanilla cook-
    and-serve pudding mix
3 tablespoons Quick Cooking
    Minute Tapioca
1 (8-ounce) can crushed
    pineapple, packed in fruit
    juice, drained, and ¼ cup
    liquid reserved
¼ cup water

1 cup unsweetened orange juice
1 (4-serving) package JELL-O
    sugar-free orange gelatin
1 (11-ounce) can mandarin
    oranges, rinsed and
    drained
¾ cup plain fat-free yogurt
⅓ cup Carnation Nonfat Dry
    Milk Powder
1 cup Cool Whip Free

In a medium saucepan, combine dry pudding mix and tapioca. Stir reserved pineapple liquid, water, and orange juice into pudding mixture. Let set for 5 minutes. Cook over medium heat until mixture thickens and starts to boil, stirring occasionally. Remove from heat. Add dry gelatin. Mix well to combine. Pour mixture into a medium bowl. Stir in pineapple and mandarin oranges. Cool for 30 minutes. In a small bowl, combine yogurt and dry milk powder. Blend in Cool Whip Free. Add yogurt mixture to tapioca mixture. Mix gently to combine. Cover and refrigerate for at least 30 minutes.

Each serving equals:

DIABETIC EXCHANGES: 1 Fruit • 1 Starch/Carbohydrate

144 Calories • 0 gm Fat • 4 gm Protein •
32 gm Carbohydrate • 165 mg Sodium •
117 mg Calcium • 1 gm Fiber

HE: 1 Fruit • ⅓ Fat Free Milk • ½ Slider •
15 Optional Calories

Orange Sherbet Salad

There's something about orange sherbet that always reminds me of the summers when I was a kid, when the bell on the ice-cream truck called us to come and enjoy! Well, you might want to invest in your own little bell, because this dish will make you feel like a kid again. *Mmm-mmm!* ◐ Serves 8

> 1 (4-serving) package JELL-O sugar-free orange gelatin
> 1 cup boiling water
> 1 cup Wells' Blue Bunny sugar- and fat-free vanilla ice cream or
>   any sugar- and fat-free ice cream
> 1 (11-ounce) can mandarin oranges, rinsed and drained
> 1 (8-ounce) can crushed pineapple, packed in fruit juice, drained
> 1 cup Cool Whip Lite
> 2 tablespoons chopped pecans

In a large bowl, combine dry gelatin and boiling water. Mix well to dissolve gelatin. Stir in ice cream, oranges, and pineapple. Pour mixture into an 8-by-8-inch dish. Refrigerate until set, about 2 hours. Spread Cool Whip Lite evenly over set gelatin and sprinkle pecans over the top. Cut into 8 servings.

Each serving equals:

DIABETIC EXCHANGES: ½ Fruit • ½ Fat •
½ Starch/Carbohydrate

86 Calories • 2 gm Fat • 2 gm Protein •
15 gm Carbohydrate • 42 mg Sodium •
39 mg Calcium • 0 gm fiber

HE: ½ Fruit • ¼ Fat • ¼ Slider

Pretty Pink Raspberry Salad

I'd serve this attractive salad at a luncheon or card party, but you don't need a special occasion to enjoy its delectable mix of flavors. If you're having difficulty finding frozen raspberries, ask your favorite store manager to order them for you. Never hesitate to ask for what you need, politely—you're worth it! ☻ Serves 6

1 (4-serving) package JELL-O sugar-free raspberry gelatin
¾ cup boiling water
¾ cup frozen unsweetened raspberries
1 (8-ounce) can crushed pineapple, packed in fruit juice,
    undrained
1 cup fat-free cottage cheese
½ cup mini marshmallows
½ cup Cool Whip Free

In a large bowl, combine dry gelatin and boiling water. Mix well to dissolve gelatin. Stir in frozen raspberries and undrained pineapple. Refrigerate for 15 minutes. Add cottage cheese and marshmallows. Mix gently to combine. Fold in Cool Whip Free. Spread mixture into an 8-by-8-inch dish. Refrigerate until firm, about 3 hours. Cut into 6 servings.

Each serving equals:

DIABETIC EXCHANGES: ½ Fruit •
½ Starch/Carbohydrate *or* 1 Starch/Carbohydrate

84 Calories • 0 gm Fat • 6 gm Protein •
15 gm Carbohydrate • 182 mg Sodium •
25 mg Calcium • 1 gm Fiber

HE: ½ Fruit • ⅓ Protein • ¼ Slider •
5 Optional Calories

Springtime Rhubarb-Strawberry Fluff Salad

Hardly anything goes better together than rhubarb and strawberries, and this is an especially luscious blend of fruit and other treats! I like to say that rhubarb is the unofficial state fruit of Iowa!

● Serves 8 (⅔ cup)

> 1 (4-serving) package JELL-O sugar-free vanilla cook-and-serve pudding mix
> 1 (4-serving) package JELL-O sugar-free strawberry gelatin
> 1 cup water
> 2 cups chopped fresh or frozen rhubarb
> 2 cups frozen unsweetened strawberries
> ¾ cup Cool Whip Free
> ½ cup mini marshmallows
> 2 tablespoons chopped pecans

In a large saucepan, combine dry pudding mix, dry gelatin, and water. Stir in rhubarb. Cook over medium heat until mixture thickens and rhubarb softens, stirring often. Stir in frozen strawberries. Place saucepan on a wire rack and allow to cool for 30 minutes. Whip on HIGH with an electric mixer until mixture is fluffy. Stir in Cool Whip Free, marshmallows, and pecans. Spoon mixture into serving bowl. Cover and refrigerate for at least 15 minutes. Gently stir again just before serving.

Each serving equals:

DIABETIC EXCHANGES: 1 Starch/Carbohydrate

69 Calories • 1 gm Fat • 1 gm Protein •
14 gm Carbohydrate • 92 mg Sodium •
33 mg Calcium • 1 gm Fiber

HE: ½ Vegetable • ¼ Fruit • ¼ Fat • ¼ Slider •
13 Optional Calories

Cranberry Fluff

So many good things go into this recipe, your taste buds will start to sing after just one bite! If you don't have a food grinder like a Cuisinart, you can also use your blender to process the cranberries. And if you can't find white grapes, experiment with red or green as long as they're seedless.   ☾   Serves 6 (¾ cup)

> 2 cups finely chopped fresh or frozen cranberries
> ½ cup Splenda Granular
> ½ cup seedless white grapes, coarsely chopped
> 1½ cups (3 small) cored, unpeeled, and diced Red Delicious
>   apples
> ½ cup mini marshmallows
> ⅓ cup chopped walnuts
> ¾ cup Cool Whip Free

In a large bowl, combine cranberries and Splenda. Cover and refrigerate for 1 hour. Add grapes, apples, marshmallows, and walnuts. Mix gently to combine. Fold in Cool Whip Free. Re-cover and refrigerate for at least 15 minutes. Gently stir again just before serving.

HINT: Slightly freeze cranberries before grinding to avoid splattering.

Each serving equals:

DIABETIC EXCHANGES: 1 Fruit • 1 Fat

108 Calories • 4 gm Fat • 1 gm Protein •
17 gm Carbohydrate • 8 mg Sodium •
11 mg Calcium • 2 gm Fiber

HE: 1 Fruit • ½ Fat • ¼ Protein • ¼ Slider •
11 Optional Calories

Pies to Make You

Believe in Magic

People ask me how I come up with so many different and delicious pies, and all I can tell them is that the ideas and the flavors just keep tumbling out on a daily basis. Sometimes, though, my inspiration comes from a friend in need.

A few years ago, I got a call from a neighbor who was going to a church potluck that very evening. It was already after 6, and she'd promised an elderly man with a heart condition that she'd bring him a strawberry cream pie.

Now here she'd hurried home from work, knowing all the time she didn't even have a recipe for one, and so she called me in hope and desperation. I created a recipe on the spot for her and told her I'd run into the kitchen and taste-test it, then call her back. (I won't ever give anyone a recipe without first making sure it works!)

Five minutes later, I called her back with a real winner!

My husband, Cliff, has been bragging about my pies since the earliest days of Healthy Exchanges, and he's convinced that someday you'll find my best ones in your supermarket's freezer case!

People now call me "the Pie Lady from Iowa," and my pies are my feature desserts wherever I go! At every cooking demonstration the pie of the day gets the most attention, and why not? Pies are the recipes most handed down from generation to generation, and a pie on the table says you've got something to celebrate, no matter how large or small. I've gotten letters from women who said that until they met up with me, they made pie only once or twice a year. Now, it's a rare week they don't fix at least one or two pies!

Here's a dream-come-true abundance of fantastic pie desserts, from irresistible cream pies in chocolate cookie crusts (*Chocolate*

Cherry Cream Pie), to fruit-filled treasures in traditional flaky crusts (*Strawberry-Glazed Pear Tarts*), to luscious combinations that recall the "off-limits" tastes of candy bars (*Rocky Road Pistachio Pie*).

Topped with "real food" treats like crunchy nuts and mini chocolate chips, these pies won't be found in other "diet" cookbooks—but you can make a piece of Healthy Exchanges pie a daily good habit—and reach your weight-loss and health goals. I'm living proof of that!

For anyone who thinks that it's too much trouble to make and eat these healthy pies, I'll tell you this: I can stir up a pie and serve it faster than you can answer the door when unexpected guests arrive!

Strawberry-Glazed Pear Tarts

Have you tried making tarts at home but never managed to give them that beautiful shiny look the bakeries do? A glaze is the secret, and here's how to give your desserts that "professional" shimmer that makes everyone's mouth water! ☻ Serves 6

> 1 (4-serving) package JELL-O sugar-free instant vanilla pudding mix
> ⅔ cup Carnation Nonfat Dry Milk Powder
> 1 cup water
> 1 (8-ounce) can sliced pears, packed in fruit juice, drained, and
>   ¼ cup liquid reserved
> 1 (6-single serve) package Keebler graham cracker crusts
> 1 (4-serving) package JELL-O sugar-free strawberry gelatin
> 2 teaspoons cornstarch
> 1 cup sliced fresh strawberries

In a medium bowl, combine dry pudding mix, dry milk powder, and water. Mix well using a wire whisk. Fold in pears. Evenly spoon mixture into graham cracker crusts. Refrigerate while preparing topping. In a medium saucepan, combine dry gelatin, cornstarch, reserved ¼ cup pear liquid, and strawberries. Cook over medium heat until mixture thickens and starts to boil, stirring constantly. Remove from heat. Place saucepan on a wire rack and cool for 10 minutes. Evenly spoon mixture over pear mixture in graham cracker crusts. Refrigerate for at least 30 minutes.

HINT: Good topped with 1 tablespoon Cool Whip Lite, but don't forget to count the few additional calories.

Each serving equals:

DIABETIC EXCHANGES: 2 Starch/Carbohydrate •
1 Fat *or* 1½ Starch/Carbohydrate • 1 Fat • ½ Fruit

---

202 Calories • 6 gm Fat • 5 gm Protein •
32 gm Carbohydrate • 450 mg Sodium •
98 mg Calcium • 2 gm Fiber

HE: 1 Bread • ½ Fruit • ½ Fat • ⅓ Fat Free Milk •
¼ Slider • 7 Optional Calories

Cherry Tarts with Chocolate Topping

I always feel a little patriotic when I serve these tarts, probably because cherries are kind of our "national fruit." (Remember George Washington and that old cherry tree?) One taste of these, and I bet I'll get your vote! ☻ Serves 6

> 1 (16-ounce) can tart red cherries, packed in water,
>   drained, and ½ cup liquid reserved
> ¾ cup water
> 1 (4-serving) package JELL-O sugar-free cherry
>   gelatin
> 1 (4-serving) package JELL-O sugar-free vanilla
>   cook-and-serve pudding mix
> 1 (6-single serve) package Keebler graham cracker
>   crusts
> ½ cup Cool Whip Free
> 1 teaspoon vanilla extract
> 1 tablespoon unsweetened cocoa
> 1 tablespoon mini chocolate chips

In a medium saucepan, combine reserved cherry liquid, water, dry gelatin, and dry pudding mix. Stir in cherries. Cook over medium heat until mixture thickens and starts to boil, stirring constantly, being careful not to crush the cherries. Remove from heat. Place saucepan on a wire rack and allow to cool for 10 minutes. Evenly spoon cherry mixture into graham cracker crusts. Refrigerate for at least 1 hour. In a small bowl, combine Cool Whip Free, vanilla extract, and cocoa. Evenly spoon mixture over cherry filling. Sprinkle ½ teaspoon chocolate chips over top of each.

Each serving equals:

DIABETIC EXCHANGES: 1 Starch/Carbohydrate • 1 Fruit • 1 Fat

195 Calories • 7 gm Fat • 3 gm Protein • 30 gm Carbohydrate • 269 mg Sodium • 11 mg Calcium • 2 gm Fiber

HE: 1 Bread • ⅔ Fruit • ½ Fat • ½ Slider • 2 Optional Calories

Becky's Peach Tarts

Remember looking in pastry shop windows and longing for those gorgeous fresh fruit tarts lined up for sale? Well, now that luscious dessert can be yours whenever you like! My daughter, Becky, could eat peaches at every meal, so when I was testing this recipe, I sent it to her husband, John, to try out on her. The verdict: Yum!

☻ Serves 6

1 (4-serving) package JELL-O sugar-free vanilla cook-and-serve
    pudding mix
1 (4-serving) package JELL-O sugar-free lemon gelatin
3 cups (6 medium) peeled and coarsely chopped fresh peaches ☆
½ cup water
¼ teaspoon ground nutmeg
1 (6-single serve) package Keebler graham cracker crusts
6 tablespoons Cool Whip Lite

In a medium saucepan, combine dry pudding mix and dry gelatin. Place 1 cup peaches and water in a blender container. Cover and process on HIGH until mixture is smooth. Pour mixture into saucepan with dry pudding and gelatin. Stir in remaining 2 cups peaches. Cook over medium heat until mixture thickens and starts to boil, stirring constantly. Remove from heat. Stir in nutmeg. Evenly spoon hot mixture into graham cracker crusts. Refrigerate for at least 2 hours. When serving, top each with 1 tablespoon Cool Whip Lite. If desired, lightly sprinkle additional nutmeg over Cool Whip Lite.

Each serving equals:

DIABETIC EXCHANGES: 1 Starch/Carbohydrate • 1 Fruit • 1 Fat

---

178 Calories • 6 gm Fat • 2 gm Protein • 29 gm Carbohydrate • 263 mg Sodium • 4 mg Calcium • 2 gm Fiber

---

HE: 1 Bread • 1 Fruit • ½ Fat • ¼ Slider • 10 Optional Calories

Heavenly Layered Lemon Pie

This is a pie of delectable contrasts: It's rich and it's light, it tastes like a calorie splurge, but you can enjoy it and still lose weight. Now if you were going to wish on a star for a luscious treat, I bet this might be the pie you'd have in mind! ☾ Serves 8

1 (8-ounce) package
  Philadelphia fat-free
  cream cheese
½ cup Cool Whip Free ☆
1 teaspoon lemon juice
2 tablespoons Splenda Granular
1 (6-ounce) Keebler shortbread
  piecrust
1 (4-serving) package JELL-O
  sugar-free instant vanilla
  pudding mix

1 (4-serving) package JELL-O
  sugar-free lemon gelatin
⅔ cup Carnation Nonfat Dry
  Milk Powder
1 (8-ounce) can crushed
  pineapple, packed in fruit
  juice, undrained
¾ cup Diet Mountain Dew
1 teaspoon coconut extract
2 tablespoons chopped pecans
2 tablespoons flaked coconut

In a medium bowl, stir cream cheese with a spoon until soft. Stir in ¼ cup Cool Whip Free, lemon juice, and Splenda. Spread mixture into piecrust. In a large bowl, combine dry pudding mix, dry gelatin, and dry milk powder. Add undrained pineapple and Diet Mountain Dew. Mix well using a wire whisk. Blend in remaining ¼ cup Cool Whip Free and coconut extract. Spread mixture evenly over cream cheese mixture. Evenly sprinkle pecans and coconut over top. Refrigerate for at least 1 hour. Cut into 8 servings.

Each serving equals:

DIABETIC EXCHANGES: 1½ Starch/Carbohydrate • 1 Fat • ½ Meat

---

211 Calories • 7 gm Fat • 8 gm Protein • 29 gm Carbohydrate • 536 mg Sodium • 74 mg Calcium • 1 gm Fiber

---

HE: 1 Bread • ½ Protein • ½ Fat • ¼ Fruit • ¼ Fat Free Milk • ½ Slider

Mint Chocolate Sundae Pie

So many lifelong dieters have handled deprivation by sneaking tastes of the desserts they crave, but here's one outrageously good meal topper you can savor to your heart's content! I want you sitting at the table instead of hiding in the kitchen—and now you can!

☻ Serves 8

> 2 cups Wells' Blue Bunny sugar- and fat-free vanilla ice cream or
>   any sugar- and fat-free ice cream
> 6 to 8 drops green food coloring ☆
> 1 teaspoon mint extract ☆
> 1 (6-ounce) Keebler chocolate piecrust
> 1 (4-serving) package JELL-O sugar-free chocolate cook-and-serve
>   pudding mix
> ⅔ cup Carnation Nonfat Dry Milk Powder
> ⅔ cup water
> ½ cup mini marshmallows
> ½ cup Cool Whip Free
> 1 tablespoon mini chocolate chips

Place ice cream in a large bowl. Let set for 10 minutes to soften. Add 4 to 6 drops green food coloring and ½ teaspoon mint extract. Mix well with sturdy spoon until mixture is combined. Spread mixture into piecrust. Cover and place in freezer while preparing chocolate sauce. Meanwhile in a medium saucepan, combine dry pudding mix, dry milk powder, and water. Cook over medium heat until mixture thickens and starts to boil, stirring constantly. Remove from heat. Stir in marshmallows. Mix well until mixture is smooth. Cool for 10 minutes. Drizzle chocolate sauce evenly over top of ice cream mixture. In a small bowl, combine Cool Whip Free, remaining ½ teaspoon mint extract, and remaining 2 to 4 drops green food coloring. Evenly drop Cool Whip Free mixture by tablespoon to form 8 mounds. Evenly sprinkle chocolate chips over mounds. Cover and freeze for at least 4 hours. Let set at room temperature for at least 15 minutes before serving. Cut into 8 servings.

Each serving equals:

DIABETIC EXCHANGES: 2 Starch/Carbohydrate • 1 Fat

210 Calories • 6 gm Fat • 6 gm Protein •
33 gm Carbohydrate • 212 mg Sodium •
129 mg Calcium • 1 gm Fiber

HE: 1 Bread • ½ Fat • ¼ Fat Free Milk • ¾ Slider •
1 Optional Calorie

Refreshing Pear Pistachio Pie

Here's a beautiful holiday season dessert that will look absolutely stunning on your buffet table. Because the ingredients are simple ones you've probably got sitting in your pantry, you can stir it up anytime—and your family will race through dinner!

◐ Serves 8

> 1 (16-ounce) can pear halves, packed in fruit juice,
>   drained, and ½ cup liquid reserved
> 1 (6-ounce) Keebler shortbread piecrust
> 1 (4-serving) package JELL-O sugar-free instant
>   vanilla pudding mix
> 1 (4-serving) package JELL-O sugar-free cherry gelatin
> 1⅓ cups Carnation Nonfat Dry Milk Powder ☆
> 1⅔ cups water ☆
> ¾ cup Cool Whip Free ☆
> 1 (4-serving) package JELL-O sugar-free instant
>   pistachio pudding mix
> 4 maraschino cherries, halved

Coarsely chop pears. Evenly arrange in bottom of piecrust. In a large bowl, combine dry vanilla pudding mix, dry gelatin, and ⅔ cup dry milk powder. Add reserved pear liquid and ⅔ cup water. Mix well using a wire whisk. Blend in ¼ cup Cool Whip Free. Spread mixture evenly over pears. Refrigerate while preparing topping. In a medium bowl, combine dry pistachio pudding mix, remaining ⅔ cup dry milk powder, and remaining 1 cup water. Mix well using a wire whisk. Blend in remaining ½ cup Cool Whip Free. Spread topping mixture evenly over cherry layer. Garnish with maraschino cherry halves. Refrigerate for at least 1 hour. Cut into 8 servings.

Each serving equals:

DIABETIC EXCHANGES: 1½ Starch/Carbohydrate •
1 Fat • ½ Fruit • ½ Fat Free Milk *or* 2 Starch/
Carbohydrate • 1 Fat • ½ Fruit

229 Calories • 5 gm Fat • 6 gm Protein •
40 gm Carbohydrate • 556 mg Sodium •
142 mg Calcium • 2 gm Fiber

HE: 1 Bread • ½ Fruit • ½ Fat Free Milk • ½ Fat •
½ Slider • 6 Optional Calories

Black Bottom Lemon Cream Pie

Here's another of my layered desserts, which are as much fun to make as they are to eat! I love the combination of chocolate and lemon, so sweet and tart, and oh-so-satisfying. ☻ Serves 8

> 1 (4-serving) package JELL-O sugar-free instant chocolate
>   pudding mix
> 1⅓ cups Carnation Nonfat Dry Milk Powder ☆
> 2¼ cups water ☆
> 1 (6-ounce) Keebler shortbread piecrust
> 1 (4-serving) package JELL-O sugar-free instant vanilla pudding
>   mix
> 1 (4-serving) package JELL-O sugar-free lemon gelatin
> ½ cup Cool Whip Free
> 1 tablespoon mini chocolate chips

In a large bowl, combine dry chocolate pudding mix, ⅔ cup dry milk powder, and 1 cup water. Mix well using a wire whisk. Spread mixture into piecrust. In another large bowl, combine dry vanilla pudding mix, dry gelatin, remaining ⅔ cup dry milk powder, and remaining 1¼ cups water. Mix well using a wire whisk. Blend in Cool Whip Free. Spread mixture evenly over chocolate layer. Evenly sprinkle chocolate chips over the top. Refrigerate for at least 1 hour. Cut into 8 servings.

Each serving equals:

DIABETIC EXCHANGES: 2 Starch/Carbohydrate • 1 Fat

189 Calories • 5 gm Fat • 6 gm Protein •
30 gm Carbohydrate • 557 mg Sodium •
139 mg Calcium • 1 gm Fiber

HE: 1 Bread • ½ Fat Free Milk • ½ Fat • ¼ Slider •
17 Optional Calories

Rocky Road Pistachio Pie

There are smooth pie lovers, and then there are people who like to find surprises in every bite: a chunk of pineapple, a chocolate chip, a bit of coconut. If you've guessed I created this pie for those "surprise lovers," you're right! ☻ Serves 8

> 1 (4-serving) package JELL-O sugar-free instant pistachio pudding
>   mix
> ⅔ cup Carnation Nonfat Dry Milk Powder
> 1 (8-ounce) can crushed pineapple, packed in fruit juice, drained,
>   and ¼ cup liquid reserved ☆
> 1 cup water
> ¾ cup Cool Whip Free ☆
> 2 tablespoons mini chocolate chips
> 1 (6-ounce) Keebler chocolate piecrust
> 1 teaspoon coconut extract
> 1 tablespoon flaked coconut

In a large bowl, combine dry pudding mix and dry milk powder. Add pineapple liquid and water. Mix well using a wire whisk. Blend in ¼ cup Cool Whip Free, chocolate chips, and half of crushed pineapple. Spread mixture into piecrust. In a small bowl, combine remaining ½ cup Cool Whip Free, remaining pineapple, and coconut extract. Frost pie with Cool Whip mixture. Sprinkle coconut evenly over the top. Refrigerate for at least 30 minutes. Cut into 8 servings.

Each serving equals:

DIABETIC EXCHANGES: 2 Starch/Carbohydrate • 1 Fat

186 Calories • 6 gm Fat • 3 gm Protein •
30 gm Carbohydrate • 297 mg Sodium •
74 mg Calcium • 1 gm Fiber

HE: 1 Bread • ½ Fat • ¼ Fat Free Milk • ¼ Fruit •
¼ Slider • 15 Optional Calories

Hawaiian Coconut Crumb Pie

Did you ever try to bash your way into a coconut fresh off the tree? That is Work with a capital W! Lucky for us, we can enjoy that delectable taste of the tropics by spooning just a bit out of a handy bag! This pie combines so many sweet flavors, your mouth will believe you're on vacation! ☻ Serves 8

1 (4-serving) package JELL-O sugar-free chocolate
    cook-and-serve pudding mix
⅔ cup Carnation Nonfat Dry Milk Powder
1 (8-ounce) can crushed pineapple, packed in fruit juice,
    undrained
1 cup water
1 teaspoon coconut extract
1 cup (1 medium) diced banana
1 (6-ounce) Keebler chocolate piecrust
6 (2½-inch)chocolate graham cracker squares
    made into fine crumbs
2 tablespoons flaked coconut
2 tablespoons chopped pecans

Preheat oven to 375 degrees. In a medium saucepan, combine dry pudding mix, dry milk powder, undrained pineapple, and water. Cook over medium heat until mixture thickens and starts to boil, stirring often. Remove from heat. Stir in coconut extract and banana. Place saucepan on a wire rack and let set for 5 minutes. Spread pudding mixture into piecrust. In a small bowl, combine graham cracker crumbs, coconut, and pecans. Evenly sprinkle crumb mixture over top. Bake for 10 to 12 minutes. Place pie plate on a wire rack and allow to cool completely. Cut into 8 servings.

HINT: To prevent banana from turning brown, mix with 1 teaspoon lemon juice or sprinkle with Fruit Fresh.

Each serving equals:

DIABETIC EXCHANGES: 1½ Starch/Carbohydrate •
1 Fat • ½ Fruit

211 Calories • 7 gm Fat • 4 gm Protein •
33 gm Carbohydrate • 206 mg Sodium •
75 mg Calcium • 1 gm Fiber

HE: 1 Bread • ¾ Fat • ½ Fruit • ¼ Fat Free Milk •
¼ Slider • 16 Optional Calories

Sunny Mandarin Orange Pie

On the grayest day of the year, when the snow's piled high or the fog has rolled in, you can brighten everyone's outlook with this delicious pie! If you're wondering why I have you rinse the mandarin oranges, it's because we still can't buy them canned in fruit juice, only light syrup. Of course, it's only a matter of time before we can, I bet!   ☻   Serves 8

2 (4-serving) packages JELL-O sugar-free instant vanilla pudding mix ☆

1 (4-serving) package JELL-O sugar-free orange gelatin

1⅓ cups Carnation Nonfat Dry Milk Powder ☆

2⅓ cups water ☆

1 (11-ounce) can mandarin oranges, rinsed and drained

1 (6-ounce) Keebler graham cracker piecrust

1 teaspoon coconut extract

½ cup Cool Whip Free

¼ cup flaked coconut ☆

In a medium bowl, combine 1 package dry pudding mix, dry gelatin, ⅔ cup dry milk powder, and 1⅓ cups water. Mix well using a wire whisk. Add mandarin oranges. Mix gently to combine. Spread mixture into piecrust. Refrigerate while preparing topping. In another medium bowl, combine remaining package dry pudding mix, remaining ⅔ cup dry milk powder, and remaining 1 cup water. Mix well using a wire whisk. Blend in coconut extract, Cool Whip Free, and 2 tablespoons coconut. Spread mixture evenly over orange filling. Evenly sprinkle remaining 2 tablespoons coconut over the top. Refrigerate for at least 1 hour. Cut into 8 servings.

Each serving equals:

DIABETIC EXCHANGES: 1½ Starch/Carbohydrate • 1 Fat • ½ Fat Free Milk

---

206 Calories • 6 gm Fat • 6 gm Protein • 32 gm Carbohydrate • 564 mg Sodium • 143 mg Calcium • 1 gm Fiber

---

HE: 1 Bread • ½ Fat Free Milk • ½ Fat • ¼ Fruit • ½ Slider • 5 Optional Calories

Rhubarb Banana Cream Delight

If you didn't grow up eating rhubarb "everything" like us native Iowans, you'll be pleased to learn that rhubarb is surprisingly easy to prepare. While it's most often blended with strawberries, my taste testers voted their approval of this combo that features banana. ◐ Serves 8

1 (4-serving) package JELL-O sugar-free vanilla cook-and-serve pudding mix

1 (4-serving) package JELL-O sugar-free strawberry gelatin

1¾ cups water ☆

2 cups chopped fresh or frozen rhubarb

1 cup (1 medium) diced banana

1 (6-ounce) Keebler shortbread piecrust

1 (4-serving) package JELL-O sugar-free instant banana cream pudding mix

⅔ cup Carnation Nonfat Dry Milk Powder

½ cup Cool Whip Free

In a medium saucepan, combine dry cook-and-serve pudding mix, dry gelatin, and ¾ cup water. Add rhubarb. Mix well to combine. Cook over medium heat until mixture thickens and rhubarb becomes soft, stirring constantly. Remove from heat. Stir in banana. Place saucepan on a wire rack and allow to cool for 10 minutes. Spoon rhubarb mixture into piecrust. Refrigerate for at least 1 hour. In a medium bowl, combine dry instant pudding mix and dry milk powder. Add remaining 1 cup water. Mix well using a wire whisk. Blend in Cool Whip Free. Spread pudding mixture evenly over rhubarb mixture. Refrigerate for at least 1 hour. Cut into 8 servings.

Each serving equals:

DIABETIC EXCHANGES: 2 Starch/Carbohydrate • ½ Fat

176 Calories • 4 gm Fat • 4 gm Protein •
31 gm Carbohydrate • 384 mg Sodium •
96 mg Calcium • 1 gm Fiber

HE: 1 Bread • ½ Vegetable • ½ Fat • ¼ Fruit •
¼ Fat Free Milk • ¼ Slider • 15 Optional Calories

Chocolate Cherry Cream Pie

This looks so lovely, with its dazzling filling of rosy cherries, you might want to turn on your camcorder and preserve it for posterity! Okay, maybe that's going a bit far, but you could take a quick Polaroid before everyone digs in and makes it disappear. And even if you don't take a single picture of it, the memory of it will last a long time! ☻ Serves 8

> 1 (4-serving) package JELL-O sugar-free chocolate
>   cook-and-serve pudding mix
> 1 (4-serving) package JELL-O sugar-free cherry
>   gelatin
> 1½ cups water ☆
> 1 (16-ounce) can tart red cherries, packed in water,
>   undrained
> 1 teaspoon almond extract
> 1 (6-ounce) Keebler chocolate piecrust
> 1 (4-serving) package JELL-O sugar-free instant chocolate
>   pudding mix
> ⅔ cup Carnation Nonfat Dry Milk Powder
> ½ cup Cool Whip Free
> 2 tablespoons slivered almonds

In a medium saucepan, combine dry cook-and-serve pudding mix, dry gelatin, and ½ cup water. Stir in undrained cherries. Cook over medium heat until mixture thickens and starts to boil, stirring often, being careful not to crush cherries. Remove from heat. Stir in almond extract. Place saucepan on a wire rack and let set for 5 minutes. Spoon cherry mixture into piecrust. Refrigerate for at least 30 minutes. Meanwhile, in a large bowl, combine dry instant pudding, dry milk powder, and remaining 1 cup water. Mix well using a wire whisk. Blend in Cool Whip Free. Spread pudding mixture evenly over cherry filling. Evenly sprinkle almonds over top. Refrigerate for at least 1 hour. Cut into 8 servings.

Each serving equals:

DIABETIC EXCHANGES: 1½ Starch/Carbohydrate •
1 Fat • ½ Fruit

---

206 Calories • 6 gm Fat • 5 gm Protein •
33 gm Carbohydrate • 385 mg Sodium •
81 mg Calcium • 1 gm Fiber

HE: 1 Bread • ½ Fruit • ½ Fat • ¼ Fat Free Milk •
½ Slider • 9 Optional Calories

Banana Split Cream Pie

Was it Mae West who first said, "Too much of a good thing is wonderful!"? (I know somebody with an appetite for life must have!) This recipe takes that quote to heart, delivering a scrumptious superstar of a dessert that's just right for a birthday or anniversary party. Who wouldn't feel special when you serve this?

● Serves 8

> 1 cup (1 medium) diced banana
> 2 cups sliced fresh strawberries
> 1 (6-ounce) Keebler graham cracker piecrust
> 1 (4-serving) package JELL-O sugar-free vanilla cook-and-serve
>   pudding mix
> 1 (4-serving) package JELL-O sugar-free strawberry gelatin
> 2 cups Diet Mountain Dew or water ☆
> 1 (4-serving) package JELL-O sugar-free instant banana cream
>   pudding mix
> ⅔ cup Carnation Nonfat Dry Milk Powder
> 1 (8-ounce) can crushed pineapple, packed in fruit juice,
>   undrained
> ½ cup Cool Whip Free
> 2 tablespoons chopped pecans

Layer banana and strawberries in bottom of piecrust. In a medium saucepan, combine dry cook-and-serve pudding mix, dry gelatin, and 1½ cups Diet Mountain Dew. Cook over medium heat until mixture thickens and starts to boil, stirring constantly. Spoon hot mixture evenly over fruit. Refrigerate for 1 hour or until set. In a medium bowl, combine dry instant pudding mix, dry milk powder, undrained pineapple, and remaining ½ cup Diet Mountain Dew. Mix well using a wire whisk. Blend in Cool Whip Free. Spread pudding mixture evenly over set filling. Sprinkle pecans evenly over top. Refrigerate for at least 30 minutes. Cut into 8 servings.

HINT: To prevent banana from turning brown, mix with 1 teaspoon lemon juice or sprinkle with Fruit Fresh.

Each serving equals:

DIABETIC EXCHANGES: 1 Starch/Carbohydrate •
1 Fruit • 1 Fat

---

170 Calories • 2 gm Fat • 5 gm Protein •
33 gm Carbohydrate • 408 mg Sodium •
92 mg Calcium • 1 gm Fiber

HE: 1 Bread • ¾ Fruit • ¾ Fat • ¼ Fat Free Milk •
¼ Slider • 150 Optional Calories

Banana Piña Colada Pie

Just as the classic rum drink transports you to a fantasy world of tropical breezes and palm trees, this delectable pie will easily convince you that you're winging your way to Paradise!

❂ Serves 8

2 cups (2 medium) diced
   bananas
1 (6-ounce) Keebler shortbread
   piecrust
1 (4-serving) package
   JELL-O sugar-free instant
   vanilla pudding mix
⅔ cup Carnation Nonfat Dry
   Milk Powder

1 (8-ounce) can crushed
   pineapple, packed in
   fruit juice, drained, and
   ¼ cup liquid reserved
¾ cup water
1 teaspoon rum extract
1½ teaspoons coconut extract ☆
1 cup Cool Whip Free ☆
2 tablespoons flaked coconut

Layer bananas in bottom of piecrust. In a medium bowl, combine dry pudding mix and dry milk powder. Add reserved pineapple liquid and water. Mix well using a wire whisk. Blend in pineapple, rum extract, 1 teaspoon coconut extract, and ¼ cup Cool Whip Free. Spread mixture evenly over bananas. Refrigerate for 15 minutes. In a small bowl, combine remaining ¾ cup Cool Whip Free and remaining ½ teaspoon coconut extract. Spread mixture evenly over set filling. Evenly sprinkle coconut over top. Refrigerate for at least 1 hour. Cut into 8 servings.

HINT: To prevent bananas from turning brown, mix with 1 teaspoon lemon juice or sprinkle with Fruit Fresh.

Each serving equals:

DIABETIC EXCHANGES: 1½ Starch/Carbohydrate •
1 Fruit • 1 Fat

218 Calories • 6 gm Fat • 3 gm Protein •
38 gm Carbohydrate • 339 mg Sodium •
76 mg Calcium • 2 gm Fiber

HE: 1 Bread • ¾ Fruit • ¼ Fat Free Milk • ¼ Slider •
11 Optional Calories

Coconut Apple Pie

There's nothing more American than apple pie, but in this country, the pursuit of happiness means having lots of choices. In this recipe, I chose to combine some traditional ingredients with a taste of wildness you won't expect. The result: a revolution in flavor whose time has surely come! ☻ Serves 8

1 (4-serving) package JELL-O
    sugar-free vanilla cook-
    and-serve pudding mix
1⅓ cups water
1½ teaspoons coconut extract ☆
1 teaspoon apple pie spice
3 cups (6 small) cored, unpeeled,
    and diced cooking apples

¼ cup raisins
1 (6-ounce) Keebler graham
    cracker piecrust
¾ cup Cool Whip Free
2 tablespoons flaked coconut

In a medium saucepan, combine dry pudding mix and water. Add 1 teaspoon coconut extract and apple pie spice. Stir in apples and raisins. Cook over medium heat until mixture thickens and apples become soft, stirring constantly. Remove from heat. Place saucepan on a wire rack and allow to cool for 10 minutes. Spread partially cooled mixture evenly into piecrust. Refrigerate for at least 1 hour. In a small bowl, combine Cool Whip Free and remaining ½ teaspoon coconut extract. Spread mixture evenly over filling. Evenly sprinkle coconut over top. Cut into 8 servings.

Each serving equals:

DIABETIC EXCHANGES: 1 Starch/Carbohydrate •
1 Fruit • 1 Fat

178 Calories • 6 gm Fat • 1 gm Protein •
30 gm Carbohydrate • 304 mg Sodium •
6 mg Calcium • 2 gm Fiber

HE: 1 Bread • 1 Fruit • ¼ Slider • 5 Optional Calories

Almond Raisin Tortoni Pie

Inspired by a classic Italian dessert, this pie provides tons of rich taste but keeps the sugar and fat content low. You'll be amazed (and your family delighted) by how much magic I can do with only a modest quantity of chopped almonds! ☻ Serves 8

8 maraschino cherries ☆
1 (4-serving) package JELL-O
    sugar-free instant vanilla
    pudding mix
⅓ cup Carnation Nonfat Dry
    Milk Powder
¾ cup water

¾ cup plain fat-free yogurt
¾ cup Cool Whip Free
1 teaspoon brandy extract
1 cup raisins
¼ cup chopped almonds
1 (6-ounce) Keebler shortbread
    piecrust

Quarter 4 maraschino cherries. Set aside. In a large bowl, combine dry pudding mix, dry milk powder, water, and yogurt. Mix well using a wire whisk. Blend in Cool Whip Free and brandy extract. Fold in raisins, almonds, and chopped maraschino cherries. Spread mixture evenly into piecrust. Cut remaining 4 maraschino cherries in half and garnish top of pie with cherry halves. Refrigerate for at least 1 hour. Cut into 8 servings.

HINT: To plump up raisins without "cooking," place in a glass measuring cup and microwave on HIGH for 45 to 60 seconds.

Each serving equals:

DIABETIC EXCHANGES: 1½ Starch/Carbohydrate •
1 Fruit • 1 Fat

---

243 Calories • 7 gm Fat • 5 gm Protein •
40 gm Carbohydrate • 338 mg Sodium •
97 mg Calcium • 2 gm Fiber

HE: 1 Bread • 1 Fruit • ½ Fat • ¼ Fat Free Milk •
½ Slider • 1 Optional Calorie

Rum Raisin Cream Pie

If it's good enough for a beloved ice cream flavor, you know it's good enough to be a Healthy Exchanges pie! I'm not sure exactly why rum and raisins make such a terrific couple, but they do. Cliff told me this one was "really, really good!"   ◐   Serves 8

> 1 (4-serving) package JELL-O sugar-free instant vanilla pudding
> mix
> ⅔ cup Carnation Nonfat Dry Milk Powder
> 1½ cups water
> 1 teaspoon rum extract
> 1 cup Cool Whip Lite ☆
> 1 cup raisins
> 1 (6-ounce) Keebler graham cracker piecrust

In a large bowl, combine dry pudding mix, dry milk powder, and water. Mix well using a wire whisk. Blend in rum extract and ¼ cup Cool Whip Lite. Add raisins. Mix well to combine. Spread pudding mixture into piecrust. Refrigerate for at least 2 hours. Cut into 8 servings. When serving, top each piece with 1 tablespoon Cool Whip Lite.

HINT: To plump up raisins without "cooking," place in a glass measuring cup and microwave on HIGH for 45 to 60 seconds.

Each serving equals:

DIABETIC EXCHANGES: 1 Starch/Carbohydrate •
1 Fruit • 1 Fat

---

214 Calories • 6 gm Fat • 4 gm Protein •
36 gm Carbohydrate • 333 mg Sodium •
78 mg Calcium • 1 gm Fiber

HE: 1 Bread • 1 Fruit • ½ Fat • ¼ Fat Free Milk •
¼ Slider • 13 Optional Calories

Pumpkin Cloud Pie

I must have had my daughter, Becky, in mind when I created this lovely dessert, because she adores butterscotch flavor, and she's a big fan of pumpkin pie. One bite is sure to send your taste buds flying high, but come down from those clouds to finish your piece (before someone else does!). ☺ Serves 8

1 (8-ounce) package Philadelphia fat-free
    cream cheese
¾ cup Cool Whip Free ☆
1 teaspoon coconut extract
1 (15-ounce) can solid-packed pumpkin
1 (4-serving) package JELL-O sugar-free instant
    butterscotch pudding mix
⅔ cup Carnation Nonfat Dry Milk Powder
¾ cup water
1 teaspoon pumpkin pie spice
1 (6-ounce) Keebler graham cracker piecrust
2 tablespoons flaked coconut
2 tablespoons chopped pecans

In a medium bowl, stir cream cheese with a spoon until soft. Add ½ cup Cool Whip Free and coconut extract. Mix gently to combine. Set aside. In a large bowl, combine pumpkin, dry pudding mix, dry milk powder, and water. Mix well using a wire whisk. Blend in pumpkin pie spice and remaining ¼ cup Cool Whip Free. Spread half of mixture into piecrust. Evenly spread cream cheese mixture over pumpkin layer, and spread remaining pumpkin mixture over cream cheese mixture. Sprinkle coconut and pecans evenly over top. Refrigerate for at least 2 hours. Cut into 8 servings.

Each serving equals:

DIABETIC EXCHANGES: 1½ Starch/Carbohydrate •
1 Fat • ½ Meat

---

216 Calories • 8 gm Fat • 8 gm Protein •
28 gm Carbohydrate • 512 mg Sodium •
86 mg Calcium • 2 gm Fiber

HE: 1 Bread • ¾ Fat • ½ Vegetable •
½ Protein • ¼ Fat Free Milk • ¼ Slider •
8 Optional Calories

Apple Pizza Pie

So many parents ask me for suggestions about what to serve at teenage parties. "They only like pizza," one woman said mournfully. "Well, then give those kids what they want," I suggested. Here's a dessert pizza that kids of all ages will just love!

◐ Serves 8

> 1 Pillsbury refrigerated unbaked 9-inch piecrust
> 3 cups (6 small) cored, unpeeled, and sliced Red Delicious apples
> ¼ cup Splenda Granular
> 1 teaspoon apple pie spice
> ¼ cup chopped pecans
> ¾ cup shredded Kraft reduced-fat Cheddar cheese

Preheat oven to 450 degrees. Place piecrust in center of 12-inch pizza pan. Let set at room temperature for 10 minutes. Press piecrust to fit pan. Evenly sprinkle apples over crust. In a small bowl, combine Splenda, apple pie spice, and pecans. Sprinkle mixture evenly over apples. Top with Cheddar cheese. Bake for 10 to 12 minutes. Cut into 8 large servings.

Each serving equals:

DIABETIC EXCHANGES: 1 Starch • 1 Fruit • 1 Fat • ½ Meat

---

186 Calories • 10 gm Fat • 4 gm Protein • 20 gm Carbohydrate • 198 mg Sodium • 81 mg Calcium • 1 gm Fiber

---

HE: 1 Bread • 1 Fat • ¾ Fruit • ½ Protein • 3 Optional Calories

Peach Crumb Pie

The filling in this all-year-round peach pie is downright mouthwatering all by itself, but when you add a crunchy crumb topping, you've served up a true winner! Just think of the wondrous aroma that will fill your kitchen while this bakes. ☯ Serves 8

> 1 Pillsbury refrigerated unbaked 9-inch piecrust
> 2 (16-ounce) cans peaches, packed in fruit juice, drained,
>   and 1 cup liquid reserved
> ¼ cup water
> 1 (4-serving) package JELL-O sugar-free vanilla cook-and-serve
>   pudding mix
> 1 (4-serving) package JELL-O sugar-free lemon gelatin
> 6 tablespoons Bisquick Reduced Fat Baking Mix
> 2 tablespoons Splenda Granular
> 2 teaspoons I Can't Believe It's Not Butter! Light margarine
> 1 tablespoon chopped pecans

Preheat oven to 375 degrees. Place piecrust in a 9-inch pie plate and flute edges. In a large saucepan, combine peach liquid, water, dry pudding mix, and dry gelatin. Mix well to combine. Coarsely chop peaches. Stir peaches into pudding mixture. Cook over medium heat until mixture thickens and starts to boil, stirring often. Spoon hot peach mixture into piecrust. In a medium bowl, combine baking mix, Splenda, and margarine. Mix well using a fork until mixture becomes crumbly. Stir in pecans. Evenly sprinkle crumb mixture over peach filling. Bake for 50 to 55 minutes. Place pie plate on a wire rack and allow to cool completely. Cut into 8 servings.

Each serving equals:

DIABETIC EXCHANGES: 1 Starch • 1 Fruit • 1 Fat

216 Calories • 8 gm Fat • 2 gm Protein •
34 gm Carbohydrate • 260 mg Sodium •
12 mg Calcium • 2 gm Fiber

HE: 1 Bread • 1 Fruit • ¾ Fat • ¼ Slider •
17 Optional Calories

Baked Peach Custard Almond Pie

Mmm, don't the words *peach* and *custard* set your mouth to watering? They sure do mine! This pie is truly old-fashioned comfort food, so sweetly fragrant you might just want to set your chair in front of the oven door and feast on the aroma while it bakes!

◐ Serves 8

> *1 Pillsbury refrigerated unbaked 9-inch piecrust*
> *3 cups (6 medium) peeled and sliced fresh peaches*
> *½ cup Splenda Granular*
> *6 tablespoons all-purpose flour*
> *½ teaspoon ground nutmeg*
> *⅔ cup Carnation Nonfat Dry Milk Powder*
> *1 cup water*
> *¼ cup sliced blanched almonds*

Preheat oven to 350 degrees. Place piecrust in a 9-inch pie plate. Flute edges and prick bottom and sides with tines of a fork. Bake 9 to 11 minutes or until lightly browned. Place pie plate on a wire rack and allow to cool completely. Evenly arrange peaches in piecrust. In a small bowl, combine Splenda, flour, nutmeg, and dry milk powder. Add water. Mix well to combine. Spread mixture evenly over peaches. Sprinkle almonds evenly over top. Bake for 50 to 60 minutes or until filling is set. Place pie plate on a wire rack and allow to cool completely. Cut into 8 servings.

Each serving equals:

DIABETIC EXCHANGES: 1 Starch/Carbohydrate • 1 Fruit • 1 Fat

---

225 Calories • 9 gm Fat • 4 gm Protein • 32 gm Carbohydrate • 135 mg Sodium • 87 mg Calcium • 2 gm Fiber

---

HE: 1 Bread • ¾ Fruit • ¾ Fat • ¼ Fat Free Milk • ¼ Slider • 11 Optional Calories

Pumpkin Pecan Crumble Pie

Does the holiday season seem to get longer each year? Now instead of beginning at Thanksgiving, it seems to start in October and last through early January! You could serve a classic pumpkin pie on every festive occasion, but why limit yourself? This version has great texture, plus lots of rich flavor to please your guests.

○ Serves 8

⅔ cup Carnation Nonfat Dry Milk Powder

¾ cup water

1 (15-ounce) can solid-packed pumpkin

½ cup + 2 tablespoons Splenda Granular ☆

2 teaspoons pumpkin pie spice

2 eggs or equivalent in egg substitute

1 (6-ounce) Keebler graham cracker piecrust

6 tablespoons purchased graham cracker crumbs or 6 (2½-inch) graham cracker squares made into crumbs

¼ cup chopped pecans

Preheat oven to 375 degrees. In a large bowl, combine dry milk powder and water. Add pumpkin, ½ cup Splenda, pumpkin pie spice, and eggs. Mix well to combine. Spread mixture into piecrust. Bake for 30 minutes. In a small bowl, combine graham cracker crumbs, pecans, and remaining 2 tablespoons Splenda. Evenly sprinkle mixture over top of pie. Continue baking for 20 to 25 minutes or until a knife inserted near the center comes out clean. Place pie plate on a wire rack and cool completely. Cut into 8 servings.

Each serving equals:

DIABETIC EXCHANGES: 1½ Starch/Carbohydrate • 1 Fat

193 Calories • 9 gm Fat • 5 gm Protein • 23 gm Carbohydrate • 185 mg Sodium • 93 mg Calcium • 2 gm Fiber

HE: 1 Bread • 1 Fat • ½ Vegetable • ¼ Fat Free Milk • ¼ Protein • ¼ Slider • 8 Optional Calories

Rhubarb Custard Pie with Strudel Topping

My grandma served just this kind of classic rhubarb cream pie to the lucky guests at her boardinghouse. Now this tummy-pleasing tradition can be passed along to a new generation when you stir this up for a potluck supper or committee meeting.

◐ Serves 8

1 Pillsbury refrigerated unbaked 9-inch piecrust
1 (4-serving) package JELL-O sugar-free vanilla cook-and-serve
   pudding mix
¾ cup water
3 cups diced fresh or frozen rhubarb
6 tablespoons Bisquick Reduced-Fat Baking Mix
2 tablespoons Splenda Granular
1 tablespoon + 1 teaspoon I Can't Believe It's Not Butter! Light
   margarine

Preheat oven to 450 degrees. Place piecrust in a 9-inch pie plate. Flute edges and prick bottom and sides with tines of a fork. Bake 9 to 11 minutes or until lightly browned. Place pie plate on a wire rack and allow to cool completely. In a large saucepan, combine dry pudding mix, water, and rhubarb. Cook over medium heat until mixture thickens and rhubarb becomes soft, stirring often. Spoon hot mixture into piecrust. In a medium bowl, combine baking mix and Splenda. Add margarine. Mix with a fork until crumbly. Evenly sprinkle mixture over top of rhubarb. Bake for 15 minutes. Lower heat to 350 degrees and continue baking for 30 minutes. Place pie plate on a wire rack and allow to cool completely. Cut into 8 servings.

Each serving equals:

DIABETIC EXCHANGES: 1½ Starch/Carbohydrate • 1 Fat

164 Calories • 8 gm Fat • 1 gm Protein •
22 gm Carbohydrate • 234 mg Sodium •
44 mg Calcium • 1 gm Fiber

HE: 1 Bread • ¾ Fat • ¾ Vegetable • ¼ Slider •
11 Optional Calories

Refreshing Rhubarb Meringue Pie

It took more than a few tries to create a delicious low-sugar meringue, but now that I've figured it out, I'm thrilled to share it with you! It's even better combined with one of my favorite fruit pies. ☺ Serves 8

> 1 Pillsbury refrigerated unbaked 9-inch piecrust
> 1 (4-serving) package JELL-O sugar-free vanilla cook-and-serve
>   pudding mix
> 1 (4-serving) package JELL-O sugar-free strawberry gelatin
> ¾ cup water
> 3 cups finely diced fresh or frozen rhubarb
> 1½ teaspoons coconut extract ☆
> 6 egg whites
> 6 tablespoons Splenda Granular
> 2 tablespoons flaked coconut

Preheat oven to 450 degrees. Place piecrust in a 9-inch pie plate. Flute edges and prick bottom and sides with tines of a fork. Bake 9 to 11 minutes or until lightly browned. Place pie plate on a wire rack and allow to cool completely. Lower heat to 350 degrees. Meanwhile, in a medium saucepan, combine dry pudding mix, dry gelatin, and water. Stir in rhubarb. Cook over medium heat until rhubarb becomes soft and mixture starts to boil, stirring often. Stir in 1 teaspoon coconut extract. Pour hot mixture into cooled piecrust. In a large bowl, beat egg whites with an electric mixer until soft peaks form. Add Splenda and remaining ½ teaspoon coconut extract. Continue beating until stiff peaks form. Spread meringue mixture evenly over filling mixture, being sure to seal to edges of piecrust. Evenly sprinkle coconut over top. Bake for 12 to 15 minutes or until meringue starts to turn golden brown. Place pie plate on a wire rack and allow to cool. Cut into 8 servings.

HINTS: 1. Egg whites beat best at room temperature.
2. Meringue pie cuts easily if you dip a sharp knife in warm water before slicing.

Each serving equals:

DIABETIC EXCHANGES: 1 Starch/Carbohydrate • 1 Fat

155 Calories • 7 gm Fat • 4 gm Protein •
19 gm Carbohydrate • 231 mg Sodium •
41 mg Calcium • 1 gm Fiber

HE: 1 Bread • ¾ Vegetable • ½ Fat • ¼ Protein •
¼ Slider • 3 Optional Calories

Cheesecakes
Even New Yorkers
Will Love

Maybe this classic dessert was made famous in the Big Apple, but out in the Midwest, we've made it our own. It's so rich, so creamy, such a perfect end to a company meal—but the ingredients in high-fat cheesecake are just too much of a good thing. I knew there had to be a way to make a low-fat cheesecake that wasn't a poor substitute, but a real dessert—and I found it!

I remember sitting with Cliff in a restaurant in Minneapolis when I spotted a magnificent-looking Black Forest cheesecake. I ate it first with my eyes, then grabbed the extra napkin on our table to jot down my ideas for making it over. (We usually eat at restaurants that use paper napkins and are already preset—we don't go into the fancy places where it's one cloth napkin per person. That extra napkin comes in handy for just such creative "emergencies"!)

When we got home, we'd no more landed in the house than I was in the kitchen re-creating that recipe—and let me tell you, it was out of this world! Now it's one of my daughter Becky's favorites, because it reminds her of the cheesecake with cherry topping her grandma McAndrews used to make.

What makes my Healthy Exchanges cheesecakes so special? Well, unlike so many "healthy" desserts, these can't be gulped down in a few seconds, leaving you ravenous for more. My cheesecakes are so substantial, so "heavy" on the sweet and creamy ingredients, that you can't eat them in big bites. In fact, I'll bet it takes even the speediest eater a good ten minutes to eat a piece of my cheesecake, since it's impossible not to savor every mouthful!

Now that fat-free cream cheese has made this delightful dream dessert a healthy reality, we can all enjoy this beloved treat as often as we like. Are you ready to go a little bit wild for *Caribbean Orange Cheesecake?* Hungry for a taste of heaven with my *Hawaiian Strawberry Paradise Cheesecake?* Or looking to celebrate any old day with *Chocolate Peanut Butter Cup Cheesecake?* Come on over, we're serving up New York's gift to the nation—it's time for CHEESECAKE!

No-Bake New York–Style Cheesecake

New Yorkers love cheesecake, and there are restaurants all over the country that actually have New York cheesecakes shipped to them overnight! Well, most of us can't afford that luxury, and now we don't have to send away for a true Big Apple taste. Just stir this one up, then sit back and revel in the applause. ☻   Serves 8

2 (8-ounce) packages Philadelphia fat-free cream cheese
1 (4-serving) package JELL-O sugar-free instant vanilla pudding mix
⅔ cup Carnation Nonfat Dry Milk Powder
1 cup water
1½ teaspoons vanilla extract
½ cup Cool Whip Free
½ cup Land O Lakes no-fat sour cream
1 (6-ounce) Keebler graham cracker piecrust
½ cup spreadable fruit (any flavor)

In a large bowl, stir cream cheese with a spoon until soft. Add dry pudding mix, dry milk powder, and water. Mix well using a wire whisk. Blend in vanilla extract, Cool Whip Free, and sour cream. Spread mixture into piecrust. Refrigerate for at least 1 hour. Cut into 8 servings. When serving, top each piece with 1 tablespoon spreadable fruit.

HINT: Spreadable fruit spreads best at room temperature.

Each serving equals:

DIABETIC EXCHANGES: 1 Starch • 1 Meat • 1 Fruit • 1 Fat

---

233 Calories • 5 gm Fat • 11 gm Protein •
36 gm Carbohydrate • 693 mg Sodium •
85 mg Calcium • 0 gm Fiber

HE: 1 Bread • 1 Protein • 1 Fruit • ½ Fat •
¼ Fat Free Milk • ¼ Slider • 15 Optional Calories

Joyful Almond Cheesecake

I've often been inspired by favorite candy bar flavors when creating exciting new desserts, so of course I wanted to invent a version of this much-loved favorite! Just as the Christmas carol promises, here's my gift to you: "tidings of comfort (food) and joy!"

◐ Serves 8

2 (8-ounce) packages
  Philadelphia fat-free
  cream cheese
1 (4-serving) package JELL-O
  sugar-free instant chocolate
  fudge pudding mix
⅔ cup Carnation Nonfat Dry
  Milk Powder
1 cup water

½ teaspoon almond extract
1½ teaspoons coconut extract ☆
1 cup Cool Whip Free ☆
1 (6-ounce) Keebler chocolate
  piecrust
2 tablespoons flaked coconut
1 tablespoon chopped almonds
1 tablespoon mini chocolate
  chips

In a large bowl, stir cream cheese with a spoon until soft. Add dry pudding mix, dry milk powder, and water. Mix well using a wire whisk. Blend in almond extract, ½ teaspoon coconut extract, and ¼ cup Cool Whip Free. Spread mixture into piecrust. Refrigerate while preparing topping. In a small bowl, combine remaining ¾ cup Cool Whip Free and remaining 1 teaspoon coconut extract. Spread mixture evenly over chocolate filling. Evenly sprinkle coconut, almonds, and chocolate chips over top. Refrigerate for at least 1 hour. Cut into 8 servings.

Each serving equals:

DIABETIC EXCHANGES: 1½ Starch/Carbohydrate •
1 Meat • 1 Fat

---

214 Calories • 6 gm Fat • 12 gm Protein •
28 gm Carbohydrate • 644 mg Sodium •
73 mg Calcium • 1 gm Fiber

HE: 1 Bread • 1 Protein • ½ Fat • ¼ Fat Free Milk •
½ Slider • 5 Optional Calories

Chocolate Peanut Butter Cup Cheesecake ❄

Goodness me, another "candy bar" cheesecake! You might be tempted to accuse me of having a one-track mind, but you'll be too busy gobbling down this splendid dish! (If you prefer creamy peanut butter to chunky, please be my guest and make the change.)

◐ Serves 8

> 1 (8-ounce) package Philadelphia fat-free
>   cream cheese
> 6 tablespoons Peter Pan reduced-fat chunky
>   peanut butter
> 1 teaspoon vanilla extract
> 1 (4-serving) package JELL-O sugar-free instant
>   vanilla pudding mix
> 1⅓ cups Carnation Nonfat Dry Milk Powder ☆
> 2 cups water ☆
> ¼ cup Cool Whip Free
> 1 (6-ounce) Keebler chocolate piecrust
> 1 (4-serving) package JELL-O sugar-free instant
>   chocolate pudding mix

In a large bowl, stir cream cheese with a spoon until soft. Blend in peanut butter and vanilla extract. Add dry vanilla pudding mix, ⅔ cup dry milk powder, and 1 cup water. Mix well using a wire whisk. Blend in Cool Whip Free. Spread mixture into piecrust. In a medium bowl, combine dry chocolate pudding mix, remaining ⅔ cup dry milk powder, and remaining 1 cup water. Mix well using a wire whisk. Spread mixture evenly over peanut butter layer. Refrigerate for at least 1 hour. Cut into 8 servings.

Each serving equals:

DIABETIC EXCHANGES: 1½ Starch/Carbohydrate •
1 Meat • 1 Fat • ½ Fat Free Milk

---

269 Calories • 9 gm Fat • 13 gm Protein •
34 mg Carbohydrate • 719 mg Sodium •
139 mg Calcium • 1 gm Fiber

HE: 1¼ Protein • 1 Bread • 1 Fat • ½ Fat Free Milk •
¼ Slider • 11 Optional Calories

Better Than Candy Cheesecake

Tommy smiled when I asked him to taste-test this recipe. Maybe it's because he loves candy bars, or maybe because he loves cheesecake. Or maybe it's just because this dessert is so tummy-pleasing it'll dazzle all the men in your life! ☻ Serves 8

2 (8-ounce) packages Philadelphia fat-free cream cheese
1 (4-serving) package JELL-O sugar-free instant chocolate fudge
pudding mix
⅔ cup Carnation Nonfat Dry Milk Powder
1 cup water
¼ cup Cool Whip Free
¼ cup Peter Pan reduced-fat peanut butter
1 (6-ounce) Keebler chocolate piecrust
2 tablespoons chopped dry-roasted peanuts
2 tablespoons fat-free caramel syrup

In a large bowl, stir cream cheese with a spoon until soft. Add dry pudding mix, dry milk powder, and water. Mix well using a wire whisk. Blend in Cool Whip Free and peanut butter. Spread mixture into piecrust. Evenly sprinkle peanuts over top. Refrigerate for at least 30 minutes. Just before serving, drizzle caramel syrup over top. Cut into 8 servings.

Each serving equals:

DIABETIC EXCHANGES: 1½ Starch/Carbohydrate •
1½ Meat • 1 Fat

---

261 Calories • 9 gm Fat • 14 gm Protein •
31 gm Carbohydrate • 692 mg Sodium •
73 mg Calcium • 1 gm Fiber

HE: 1⅔ Protein • 1 Bread • 1 Fat • ¼ Fat Free Milk •
¼ Slider • 6 Optional Calories

Faux Tiramisu Cheesecake

Over the years, I've tasted hundreds of desserts with my eyes and my imagination. Knowing the ingredients is usually enough for me to create my own version of something wonderful. This recipe was inspired by an exquisite Italian confection that is the chosen dessert of true romantics. Isn't love grand?　❤　Serves 8

2 (8-ounce) packages Philadelphia fat-free cream cheese
1 (4-serving) package JELL-O sugar-free instant vanilla pudding mix
⅔ cup Carnation Nonfat Dry Milk Powder
1 cup cold coffee
1 teaspoon brandy extract
¾ cup Cool Whip Lite ☆
1 (6-ounce) Keebler chocolate piecrust
2 tablespoons mini chocolate chips

In a large bowl, stir cream cheese with a spoon until soft. Add dry pudding mix, dry milk powder, and coffee. Mix well using a wire whisk. Blend in brandy extract, and ¼ cup Cool Whip Lite. Spread mixture into piecrust. Evenly drop remaining Cool Whip Lite by tablespoon to form 8 mounds. Sprinkle chocolate chips over top. Refrigerate for at least 1 hour. Cut into 8 servings.

Each serving equals:

DIABETIC EXCHANGES: 1½ Starch/Carbohydrate • 1 Meat • 1 Fat

207 Calories • 7 gm Fat • 11 gm Protein • 25 gm Carbohydrate • 636 mg Sodium • 71 mg Calcium • 1 gm Fiber

HE: 1 Bread • 1 Protein • ½ Fat • ¼ Fat Free Milk • ¼ Slider • 17 Optional Calories

Chocolate Chip Cheesecake

Here's a simply elegant delight that makes a classic cheesecake sparkle just that much more! It doesn't take a lot of chocolate to make a chocolate lover's heart beat faster, and when it's coupled with a luscious vanilla cheesecake—watch out!

● Serves 8

2 (8-ounce) packages Philadelphia fat-free cream cheese
1 (4-serving) package JELL-O sugar-free instant vanilla pudding mix
⅔ cup Carnation Nonfat Dry Milk Powder
1 cup water
1 cup Cool Whip Lite ☆
1 teaspoon vanilla extract
¼ cup mini chocolate chips ☆
1 (6-ounce) Keebler chocolate piecrust

In a large bowl, stir cream cheese with a spoon until soft. Add dry pudding mix, dry milk powder, and water. Mix well using a wire whisk. Blend in ¼ cup Cool Whip Lite, vanilla extract, and 3 tablespoons chocolate chips. Spread mixture into piecrust. Evenly spread remaining ¾ cup Cool Whip Lite over filling and sprinkle remaining 1 tablespoon chocolate chips over top. Refrigerate for at least 1 hour. Cut into 8 servings.

Each serving equals:

DIABETIC EXCHANGES: 1½ Starch/Carbohydrate •
1 Meat • 1 Fat

224 Calories • 8 gm Fat • 11 gm Protein •
27 gm Carbohydrate • 636 mg Sodium •
71 mg Calcium • 1 gm Fiber

HE: 1 Bread • 1 Protein • ½ Fat • ¼ Fat Free Milk •
½ Slider • 11 Optional Calories

Rocky Road Cheesecake

Talk about a man-pleaser! This recipe is so chock-full of goodies, you might just get anything you want from the man in your life after you serve him this outrageous treat! (I won't tell you what I asked Cliff for, but he said "Yes!") ◐ Serves 8

> 2 (8-ounce) packages Philadelphia fat-free cream cheese
> 1 (4-serving) package JELL-O sugar-free instant chocolate
>   pudding mix
> ⅔ cup Carnation Nonfat Dry Milk Powder
> 1 cup water
> 1 teaspoon vanilla extract
> ¼ cup Cool Whip Free
> 1 (6-ounce) Keebler graham cracker piecrust
> ½ cup mini marshmallows
> 2 tablespoons mini chocolate chips
> ¼ cup chopped dry-roasted peanuts

Preheat oven to 415 degrees. In a large bowl, stir cream cheese with a spoon until soft. Add dry pudding mix, dry milk powder, and water. Mix well using a wire whisk. Blend in vanilla extract and Cool Whip Free. Spread mixture into piecrust. Evenly sprinkle marshmallows, chocolate chips, and peanuts over top. Bake for 5 minutes or until marshmallows start to turn brown. Refrigerate for at least 1 hour. Cut into 8 servings.

Each serving equals:

DIABETIC EXCHANGES: 2 Starch/Carbohydrate •
1 Meat • 1 Fat

240 Calories • 8 gm Fat • 13 gm Protein •
29 gm Carbohydrate • 674 mg Sodium •
73 mg Calcium • 1 gm Fiber

HE: 1 Bread • 1 Protein • ¾ Fat • ¼ Fat Free Milk •
½ Slider • 2 Optional Calories

Maple Crunch Cheesecake

Our kitchen staff had lots of fun preparing and tasting this unusual recipe that's inspired by maple sugaring time in New England. It'll warm your heart and soothe your soul with every single bite!

◐ Serves 8

> 2 (8-ounce) packages Philadelphia fat-free cream cheese
> 1 (4-serving) package JELL-O sugar-free instant vanilla pudding mix
> ⅔ cup Carnation Nonfat Dry Milk Powder
> 1 cup Log Cabin's Sugar Free Maple Syrup
> ¼ cup Cool Whip Free
> 1 cup Healthy Choice Almond Crunch Cereal with Raisins ☆
> 1 (6-ounce) Keebler graham cracker piecrust
> 2 tablespoons chopped pecans

In a large bowl, stir cream cheese with a spoon until soft. Add dry pudding mix, dry milk powder, and maple syrup. Mix well using a wire whisk. Blend in Cool Whip Free. Gently stir in ¾ cup Almond Crunch. Spread mixture into piecrust. Evenly sprinkle remaining ¼ cup Almond Crunch and pecans over top. Refrigerate for at least 1 hour. Cut into 8 servings.

Each serving equals:

DIABETIC EXCHANGES: 2 Starch/Carbohydrate •
1 Meat • 1 Fat

238 Calories • 6 gm Fat • 12 gm Protein •
34 gm Carbohydrate • 777 mg Sodium •
72 mg Calcium • 1 gm Fiber

HE: 1 Bread • 1 Protein • ¾ Fat • ¼ Fat Free Milk •
½ Slider • 16 Optional Calories

Strawberry Fields Cheesecake

The Beatles invited us to spend forever in Strawberry Fields, and if you could enjoy this sweet and scrumptious cheesecake often, you might just accept their invitation. And anyone who knows me knows just how much I adore strawberries, so don't be surprised if I open a branch of JO's Cafe there! ☻ Serves 8

2 (8-ounce) packages Philadelphia fat-free cream cheese
1 (4-serving) package JELL-O sugar-free instant vanilla pudding mix
⅔ cup Carnation Nonfat Dry Milk Powder
1 cup water
½ cup Cool Whip Free ☆
1 (6-ounce) Keebler graham cracker piecrust
⅓ cup Land O Lakes no-fat sour cream
2 cups sliced fresh strawberries
¼ cup strawberry spreadable fruit

In a large bowl, stir cream cheese with a spoon until soft. Add dry pudding mix, dry milk powder, and water. Mix well using a wire whisk. Blend in ¼ cup Cool Whip Free. Spread mixture into piecrust. In a small bowl, combine sour cream and remaining ¼ cup Cool Whip Free. Spread mixture evenly over filling. Evenly arrange strawberries over top. In a small glass bowl, microwave strawberry spreadable fruit on HIGH for 30 seconds. Drizzle hot spreadable fruit evenly over strawberries. Refrigerate for at least 1 hour. Cut into 8 servings.

Each serving equals:

DIABETIC EXCHANGES: 1 Starch/Carbohydrate •
1 Meat • 1 Fruit • 1 Fat

---

225 Calories • 5 gm Fat • 12 gm Protein •
33 gm Carbohydrate • 687 mg Sodium •
85 mg Calcium • 1 gm Fiber

HE: 1 Bread • 1 Protein • ¾ Fruit • ½ Fat •
¼ Fat Free Milk • ¼ Slider • 10 Optional Calories

Heavenly Blueberry Orange Cheesecake

Orange and blue are at opposite ends of the color spectrum, but the contrast is very eye-catching. Mingling those "opposite" flavors in this beautiful cheesecake will invite your taste buds to dance in delight.   ◐   Serves 8

2 (8-ounce) packages Philadelphia fat-free
    cream cheese
1 (4-serving) package JELL-O sugar-free instant
    vanilla pudding mix
1 (4-serving) package JELL-O sugar-free orange
    gelatin
⅔ cup Carnation Nonfat Dry Milk Powder
1 cup Diet Mountain Dew
1 (11-ounce) can mandarin oranges, rinsed and
    drained ☆
¾ cup Cool Whip Free ☆
1 (6-ounce) Keebler graham cracker piecrust
6 tablespoons blueberry spreadable fruit
1 teaspoon coconut extract
2 tablespoons flaked coconut

In a large bowl, stir cream cheese with a spoon until soft. Add dry pudding mix, dry gelatin, dry milk powder, and Diet Mountain Dew. Mix well using a wire whisk. Reserve 8 orange pieces. Blend in remaining mandarin oranges and ¼ cup Cool Whip Free. Spread mixture into piecrust. Refrigerate while preparing topping. In a small bowl, combine spreadable fruit and coconut extract. Fold in remaining ½ cup Cool Whip Free. Spread mixture evenly over filling. Sprinkle coconut evenly over topping. Arrange reserved orange pieces evenly over top. Refrigerate for at least 1 hour. Cut into 8 servings.

Each serving equals:

DIABETIC EXCHANGES: 1 Starch/Carbohydrate •
1 Meat • 1 Fruit • 1 Fat

237 Calories • 5 gm Fat • 12 gm Protein •
36 gm Carbohydrate • 709 mg Sodium •
73 mg Calcium • 1 gm Fiber

HE: 1 Bread • 1 Protein • 1 Fruit • ½ Fat •
¼ Fat Free Milk • ¼ Slider • 13 Optional Calories

Caribbean Orange Cheesecake

Cliff and I went cruising in the islands quite a few years ago, and it was such a wonderful experience, we've often dreamed of going back—and maybe bringing along a few friends to share the journey! But even if you can't join us on our Healthy Exchanges cruise, you'll be part of the party when you mix up this flavorful cheesecake. ☻ Serves 8

> 2 (8-ounce) packages Philadelphia fat-free cream cheese
> 1 (4-serving) package JELL-O sugar-free instant vanilla pudding mix
> 1 (4-serving) package JELL-O sugar-free orange gelatin
> ⅔ cup Carnation Nonfat Dry Milk Powder
> 1 cup Diet Mountain Dew
> 1 cup Cool Whip Free ☆
> 1 (6-ounce) Keebler graham cracker piecrust
> 1 (8-ounce) can crushed pineapple, packed in fruit juice, well drained
> 1 teaspoon coconut extract
> 1 teaspoon rum extract
> 2 tablespoons flaked coconut
> 2 tablespoons chopped pecans

In a large bowl, stir cream cheese with a spoon until soft. Add dry pudding mix, dry gelatin, and dry milk powder. Add Diet Mountain Dew. Mix well using a wire whisk. Blend in ¼ cup Cool Whip Free. Spread mixture evenly into piecrust. Refrigerate while preparing topping. In a medium bowl, combine pineapple and remaining ¾ cup Cool Whip Free. Blend in coconut extract and rum extract. Spread topping mixture evenly over cream cheese filling. Evenly sprinkle coconut and pecans over top. Refrigerate for at least 30 minutes. Cut into 8 servings.

Each serving equals:

DIABETIC EXCHANGES: 2 Starch/Carbohydrate •
1 Meat • 1 Fat

---

230 Calories • 6 gm Fat • 12 gm Protein •
32 gm Carbohydrate • 709 mg Sodium •
74 mg Calcium • 1 gm Fiber

HE: 1 Bread • 1 Protein • ¾ Fat • ¼ Fat Free Milk •
¼ Fruit • ¼ Slider • 16 Optional Calories

Cherries Jubilee Cheesecake

I grew up at a time when fancy desserts meant Baked Alaska or maybe this glorious celebration of cherries! This recipe is wonderful for showing your guests how thrilled you are to be breaking bread together on this special night. ☻ Serves 8

> 2 (8-ounce) packages Philadelphia fat-free cream cheese
> 1 (4-serving) package JELL-O sugar-free instant vanilla pudding mix
> ⅔ cup Carnation Nonfat Dry Milk Powder
> 1 cup water
> ¾ cup Cool Whip Lite ☆
> 1 teaspoon brandy extract
> 3 to 4 drops red food coloring
> 2 cups pitted bing or sweet cherries
> 1 (6-ounce) Keebler shortbread piecrust

In a large bowl, stir cream cheese with a spoon until soft. Add dry pudding mix, dry milk powder, and water. Mix well using a wire whisk. Blend in ¼ cup Cool Whip Lite, brandy extract, and red food coloring. Add cherries. Mix gently to combine. Spread mixture into piecrust. Refrigerate for at least 1 hour. Cut into 8 servings. When serving, top each with 1 tablespoon Cool Whip Lite.

HINT: A 16-ounce can pitted bing cherries, rinsed and drained, may be substituted for fresh cherries.

Each serving equals:

DIABETIC EXCHANGES: 1½ Starch/Carbohydrate • 1 Meat • 1 Fat • ½ Fruit

214 Calories • 6 gm Fat • 11 gm Protein • 29 gm Carbohydrate • 671 mg Sodium • 75 mg Calcium • 1 gm Fiber

HE: 1 Bread • 1 Protein • ½ Fat • ½ Fruit • ¼ Fat Free Milk • ¼ Slider • 4 Optional Calories

Almond Black Forest Cheesecake

Creating fabulous healthy dessert recipes is probably my favorite part of my job, and why wouldn't it be, when I can blend some of my best-loved ingredients into a festive celebration of flavors! If you've never tried black cherry spreadable fruit, *ooh*, have you got something tasty in store.　　◐　Serves 8

> 2 (8-ounce) packages Philadelphia fat-free cream cheese
> 1 (4-serving) package JELL-O sugar-free instant chocolate fudge
>   pudding mix
> ⅔ cup Carnation Nonfat Dry Milk Powder
> 1 cup water
> 1 teaspoon almond extract ☆
> ¾ cup Cool Whip Free ☆
> 1 (6-ounce) Keebler chocolate piecrust
> ½ cup black cherry spreadable fruit
> 2 tablespoons chopped almonds

In a large bowl, stir cream cheese with a spoon until soft. Add dry pudding mix, dry milk powder, and water. Mix well using a wire whisk. Blend in ½ teaspoon almond extract and ¼ cup Cool Whip Free. Spread mixture into piecrust. Refrigerate while preparing topping. In a small bowl, combine spreadable fruit and remaining ½ teaspoon almond extract. Fold in remaining ½ cup Cool Whip Free. Spread mixture evenly over chocolate layer. Evenly sprinkle almonds over top. Refrigerate for at least 1 hour. Cut into 8 servings.

Each serving equals:

DIABETIC EXCHANGES: 1 Starch/Carbohydrate •
1 Meat • 1 Fruit • 1 Fat

---

246 Calories • 6 gm Fat • 12 gm Protein •
36 gm Carbohydrate • 640 mg Sodium •
75 mg Calcium • 1 gm Fiber

HE: 1 Bread • 1 Protein • 1 Fruit • ½ Fat •
¼ Fat Free Milk • ¼ Slider • 18 Optional Calories

Peach Melba Cheesecake

I don't have the research to prove it, but I'd bet that cheesecake is the most-often chosen restaurant dessert in America! This version is dazzling with its glorious abundance of fresh peaches and fresh raspberries. It's special enough to serve at a wedding reception or graduation party, but you're special enough to enjoy it anytime at all!   ◐   Serves 8

2 (8-ounce) packages Philadelphia fat-free cream cheese
1 (4-serving) package JELL-O sugar-free instant vanilla pudding
   mix
²⁄₃ cup Carnation Nonfat Dry Milk Powder
1 cup Diet Rite white grape soda
¼ cup Cool Whip Free
1 (6-ounce) Keebler shortbread piecrust
1½ cups (3 medium) peeled and chopped fresh peaches
⅓ cup water
1 (4-serving) package JELL-O sugar-free raspberry gelatin
¾ cup fresh red raspberries

In a medium bowl, stir cream cheese with a spoon until soft. Add dry pudding mix, dry milk powder, and white grape soda. Mix well using a wire whisk. Blend in Cool Whip Free. Spread mixture into piecrust. Refrigerate while preparing topping. In a medium saucepan, combine peaches and water. Cook over medium heat until peaches are soft and mixture starts to boil, stirring often. Remove from heat. Stir in dry gelatin. Mix well to dissolve gelatin. Gently fold in raspberries. Refrigerate for 20 minutes. Evenly spoon over cheesecake layer. Refrigerate for at least 2 hours. Cut into 8 servings.

HINT: 1 cup water may be used in place of Diet Rite white grape
       soda.

Each serving equals:

DIABETIC EXCHANGES: 1 Starch/Carbohydrate •
1 Meat • 1 Fat • ½ Fruit

---

213 Calories • 5 gm Fat • 12 gm Protein •
30 gm Carbohydrate • 706 mg Sodium •
73 mg Calcium • 2 gm Fiber

HE: 1 Bread • 1 Protein • ½ Fruit • ½ Fat •
¼ Fat Free Milk • ¼ Slider • 2 Optional Calories

Cranberry Holiday Cheesecake

What could be more festive for an evening of carol singing around the piano or tree trimming in the den? The walnuts add just the right amount of crunch to this tart and fruity, creamy rich cake. You might have started with "Silent Night," but your friends will soon be offering noisy thanks!   ☻   Serves 8

> 1 (4-serving) package JELL-O sugar-free cook-and-serve vanilla
>   pudding mix
> 2 cups Ocean Spray reduced-calorie cranberry juice cocktail ☆
> 2 cups fresh or frozen cranberries
> 2 (8-ounce) packages Philadelphia fat-free cream cheese
> 1 (4-serving) package JELL-O sugar-free instant vanilla pudding
>   mix
> ⅔ cup Carnation Nonfat Dry Milk Powder
> ¾ cup Cool Whip Lite ☆
> 4 to 5 drops red food coloring
> 1 (6-ounce) Keebler graham cracker piecrust
> 2 tablespoons chopped walnuts

In a medium saucepan, combine dry cook-and-serve pudding mix and 1 cup cranberry juice cocktail. Stir in cranberries. Cook over medium heat until mixture thickens and cranberries become soft, stirring constantly. Remove from heat and place saucepan on a wire rack to cool for 15 minutes. In a large bowl, stir cream cheese with a spoon until soft. Add dry instant pudding mix, dry milk powder, and remaining 1 cup cranberry juice cocktail. Mix well using a wire whisk. Blend in ¼ cup Cool Whip Lite and red food coloring. Spread mixture into piecrust. Spread cooled cranberry mixture evenly over top of cream cheese mixture. Evenly sprinkle walnuts over top. Refrigerate for at least 1 hour. Cut into 8 servings. When serving, top each piece with 1 tablespoon Cool Whip Lite.

Each serving equals:

DIABETIC EXCHANGES: 1½ Starch/Carbohydrate •
1 Meat • 1 Fat • ½ Fruit

---

235 Calories • 7 gm Fat • 11 gm Protein •
32 gm Carbohydrate • 737 mg Sodium •
73 mg Calcium • 1 gm Fiber

HE: 1 Bread • 1 Protein • ½ Fruit • ½ Fat •
¼ Fat Free Milk • ½ Slider • 6 Optional Calories

Holiday Pumpkin Cheesecake

If you're heading for your in-laws' this holiday season, and you want to make a splash, why not prepare an untraditional pumpkin pie that's truly special? I'm confident your family won't ever have tasted a richer pumpkin dessert, but be prepared to be disbelieved when you inform them after dinner that the cheesecake they loved is a healthy one! ◐ Serves 8

> 2 (8-ounce) packages Philadelphia fat-free cream cheese
> 1 (4-serving) package JELL-O sugar-free instant butterscotch pudding mix
> ⅔ cup Carnation Nonfat Dry Milk Powder
> 1 (15-ounce) can solid-packed pumpkin
> 1½ teaspoons pumpkin pie spice
> ¾ cup Cool Whip Lite ☆
> 1 (6-ounce) Keebler graham cracker piecrust
> 2 tablespoons chopped pecans

In a large bowl, stir cream cheese with a spoon until soft. Add dry pudding mix, dry milk powder, pumpkin, and pumpkin pie spice. Mix well using a wire whisk. Blend in ¼ cup Cool Whip Lite. Spread mixture into piecrust. Evenly spread remaining ½ cup Cool Whip Lite over filling. Evenly sprinkle pecans over top. Refrigerate for at least 2 hours. Cut into 8 servings.

Each serving equals:

DIABETIC EXCHANGES: 2 Starch/Carbohydrate •
1 Meat • 1 Fat

---

227 Calories • 7 gm Fat • 12 gm Protein •
29 gm Carbohydrate • 679 mg Sodium •
89 mg Calcium • 3 gm Fiber

HE: 1 Bread • 1 Protein • ¾ Fat • ½ Vegetable •
¼ Fat Free Milk • ¼ Slider • 8 Optional Calories

Dreamy, Creamy

Cakes

My husband, Cliff, is the king of spice cakes, so when I want something from him and sweet-talking just won't do the trick, I hustle out to the kitchen and stir up a spice cake recipe just for him! I know he loves the taste, but he also enjoys the sweet memories of how his grandma fussed over him and baked up his favorite. He loves the raisins and cinnamon combination (most men do, I'll bet!) and when you add a little allspice and turn that oven on—stand back! Talk about a kitchen aphrodisiac. . . .

To this day, spice cake is what I always make for Cliff's birthday. He looks forward to it just like a little kid. (Well, sometimes I make him a raisin pie—I wouldn't want to get predictable. Gotta keep him on his toes!) There's something so wonderfully warm and cozy about homemade cake, especially when the occasion is special and the person you're baking for is someone you really care about.

Ladies, here's my advice: Forget about expensive perfume, just sprinkle on some cinnamon and bake your loved one a healthy, tasty cake.

When the goal is short-term weight loss, maybe you can live with knowing that the kind of desserts you truly love are off-limits for the duration. But what if the duration is the rest of your life? Is it humanly possible to give up cake . . . forever? Maybe it is, but it's not what I'd call living a good life when you deny yourself something you relish.

Here's the good news: Healthy Exchanges cakes (like *Bananas Foster Upside-Down Cake* and *Mocha Raisin Cake*) will make your taste buds sit up and sing. They're full of the flavors you love, not dry and tasteless as so many fat-free desserts seem to be. One of the

117

most popular categories for recipe makeovers in my newsletter is cakes, especially beloved family favorites that deliver wonderful memories along with too much fat and sugar.

Let's keep the good memories alive but find ways to replace the extra sugar and fat. Figuring out how to do it is a challenge for me sometimes, but once I've "figured it out," you'll find that making them is "a piece of cake"!

With Healthy Exchanges, *you can have your cake and eat it, too.*

Cliff's Crazy Cake

When I first started creating Healthy Exchanges recipes, I found lots of inspiration in the flavors my husband, Cliff, liked best. What's more, I still do! This cake combines some surprising ingredients, but together they produce a tasty treat that will truly drive the people you love best C-R-A-Z-Y (in a good way)!

❤ Serves 8

1½ cups all-purpose flour
1½ teaspoons baking soda
3 tablespoons unsweetened
    cocoa
½ cup Splenda Granular
1 cup water
2 teaspoons vanilla extract
1 tablespoon + 1 teaspoon
    vegetable oil

1 tablespoon vinegar
2 tablespoons mini chocolate
    chips
2 tablespoons chopped
    pecans
½ cup mini marshmallows

Preheat oven to 350 degrees. Spray an 8-by-8-inch baking dish with butter-flavored cooking spray. In a medium bowl, combine flour, baking soda, cocoa, and Splenda. Add water, vanilla extract, oil, and vinegar. Stir just to combine. Spread batter into prepared baking dish. Evenly sprinkle chocolate chips, pecans, and marshmallows over top. Bake for 25 to 30 minutes. Place baking dish on a wire rack and allow to cool completely. Cut into 8 servings.

Each serving equals:

DIABETIC EXCHANGES: 1½ Starch/Carbohydrate •
½ Fruit

144 Calories • 4 gm Fat • 3 gm Protein •
24 gm Carbohydrate • 370 mg Sodium •
8 mg Calcium • 2 gm Fiber

HE: 1 Bread • ¾ Fat • ¼ Slider • 7 Optional Calories

Mexican Orange Mocha Torte

Sometimes just a touch of spice can take you on a delicious journey to a land of exotic flavors and endless sunshine.

● Serves 8

1½ cups all-purpose flour
¼ cup unsweetened cocoa
¼ cup Splenda Granular
1 teaspoon baking powder
½ teaspoon baking soda
1 teaspoon ground cinnamon
1½ teaspoons instant coffee
   crystals ☆
⅓ cup plain fat-free yogurt
½ cup Kraft fat-free
   mayonnaise

2½ cups water
2 (4-serving) packages JELL-O
   sugar-free instant
   chocolate fudge pudding
   mix ☆
1⅓ cups Carnation Nonfat
   Dry Milk Powder ☆
1 (11-ounce) can mandarin
   oranges, rinsed
½ cup Cool Whip Free

Preheat oven to 350 degrees. Spray two 9-inch round cake pans with butter-flavored cooking spray. In a large bowl, combine flour, cocoa, Splenda, baking powder, baking soda, cinnamon, and 1 teaspoon coffee crystals. In a medium bowl, combine yogurt, mayonnaise, and ½ cup water. Add yogurt mixture to flour mixture. Mix gently to combine. Evenly spread batter into prepared cake pans. Bake for 18 to 22 minutes or until a toothpick inserted in center comes out clean. Place cake pans on wire racks and cool for 10 minutes. Remove cakes from pans and continue to cool completely on wire racks. Place 1 cake on cake serving plate. In a medium bowl, combine 1 package dry pudding mix, ⅔ cup dry milk powder, and 1 cup water. Mix well using a wire whisk. Fold in mandarin oranges. Evenly spread pudding mixture over bottom layer of cooled cake. Arrange second cake over pudding mixture. In the same bowl, combine remaining package dry pudding mix, remaining ⅔ cup dry milk powder, remaining ½ teaspoon dry coffee crystals, and remaining 1 cup water. Mix well using a wire whisk. Blend in Cool Whip Free. Spread mixture evenly over top of cake. Refrigerate for at least 10 minutes. Cut into 8 servings. Refrigerate leftovers.

Each serving equals:

DIABETIC EXCHANGES: 2 Starch/Carbohydrate •
½ Fat Free Milk

209 Calories • 1 gm Fat • 8 gm Protein •
42 gm Carbohydrate • 753 mg Sodium •
206 mg Calcium • 2 gm Fiber

HE: 1 Bread • ½ Fat Free Milk • ¼ Fruit • ½ Slider •
7 Optional Calories

Cranapple Walnut Cake

Talk about perfect partnerships, and you've got to mention cranberries and apples! Just as on the best teams, each makes the other better. Toss in some crunchy walnuts, and you've got a splendid cake to savor all through the fall!   ☻   Serves 8

1 cup + 2 tablespoons all-
　　purpose flour
1 (4-serving) package JELL-O
　　sugar-free instant vanilla
　　pudding mix
1 teaspoon apple pie spice
2 tablespoons Splenda
　　Granular
1 teaspoon baking soda
½ cup coarsely chopped fresh
　　or frozen cranberries

2 cups (4 small) cored,
　　unpeeled, and finely
　　chopped cooking apples
¼ cup chopped walnuts
½ cup Ocean Spray reduced-
　　calorie cranberry juice
　　cocktail
1 egg or equivalent in egg
　　substitute
½ cup unsweetened applesauce

Preheat oven to 350 degrees. Spray an 8-by-8-inch baking dish with butter-flavored cooking spray. In a large bowl, combine flour, dry pudding mix, apple pie spice, Splenda, and baking soda. Stir in cranberries, apples, and walnuts. In a small bowl, combine cranberry juice cocktail, egg, and applesauce. Add liquid mixture to flour mixture. Mix gently to combine. Spread batter evenly into prepared baking dish. Bake for 45 to 50 minutes or until a toothpick inserted in center comes out clean. Place baking dish on a wire rack and allow to cool. Cut into 8 servings.

HINT: Good served warm with Wells' Blue Bunny sugar- and fat-free ice cream or cold with Cool Whip Lite.

Each serving equals:

DIABETIC EXCHANGES: 1 Fruit • ½ Starch • ½ Fat

139 Calories • 3 gm Fat • 3 gm Protein •
25 gm Carbohydrate • 333 mg Sodium •
12 mg Calcium • 2 gm Fiber

HE: ¾ Bread • ¾ Fruit • ¼ Fat • ¼ Protein •
14 Optional Calories

Lemon Cake

Maybe I should have called this Lemon Lemon Cake, because each of its two layers is so lemony! Make sure you only use white vinegar in this recipe (and wherever it's called for) as other kinds of vinegar won't deliver the taste you're looking for.　●　Serves 12

1⅓ cups Carnation Nonfat
　　Dry Milk Powder ☆
1 cup cold water
2 teaspoons white vinegar
1½ cups all-purpose flour
2 (4-serving) packages
　　JELL-O sugar-free
　　lemon gelatin ☆
½ cup Splenda Granular
1 teaspoon baking powder

½ teaspoon baking soda
⅓ cup Kraft fat-free
　　mayonnaise
⅓ cup plain fat-free yogurt
1 tablespoon vanilla extract ☆
1 (4-serving) package JELL-O
　　sugar-free instant vanilla
　　pudding mix
1 cup Diet Mountain Dew
¾ cup Cool Whip Free

Preheat oven to 350 degrees. Spray a 9-by-9-inch cake pan with butter-flavored cooking spray. In a small bowl, combine ⅔ cup dry milk powder, water, and vinegar. Set aside. In a large bowl, combine flour, 1 package dry gelatin, Splenda, baking powder, and baking soda. Add mayonnaise, yogurt, and 2 teaspoons vanilla extract to milk mixture. Mix gently to combine. Blend into flour mixture. Spread batter into prepared cake pan. Bake for 25 to 30 minutes or until a toothpick inserted in center comes out clean. Place cake pan on a wire rack and allow to cool for 30 minutes. In a large bowl, combine remaining package dry gelatin, dry pudding mix, remaining ⅔ cup dry milk powder, and Diet Mountain Dew. Blend in Cool Whip Free and remaining 1 teaspoon vanilla extract. Spread mixture evenly over cake. Refrigerate for at least 30 minutes. Cut into 12 servings. Refrigerate leftovers.

Each serving equals:

DIABETIC EXCHANGES: 1½ Starch/Carbohydrate

112 Calories • 0 gm Fat • 6 gm Protein •
22 gm Carbohydrate • 400 mg Sodium •
130 mg Calcium • 1 gm Fiber

HE: ⅔ Bread • ⅓ Fat Free Milk • ¼ Slider •
13 Optional Calories

Strawberry Surprise Cake

This concoction starring my gem of fruits was a winter season inspiration. How do I know? Because it calls for frozen strawberries instead of fresh! I made this for James and Pam and the boys when they came to visit, and I learned something important: You're never too old or too young to enjoy a tasty surprise. ☻ Serves 8

½ cup mini marshmallows
1½ cups all-purpose flour
1 (4-serving) package JELL-O
    sugar-free instant vanilla
    pudding mix
½ cup Splenda Granular
2 teaspoons baking powder
½ teaspoon baking soda
¾ cup plain fat-free yogurt
⅓ cup Carnation Nonfat Dry
    Milk Powder

1 egg or equivalent in egg
    substitute
¼ cup water
1 teaspoon vanilla extract
2 cups frozen unsweetened
    strawberries, thawed,
    coarsely chopped, and
    undrained
1 (4-serving) package JELL-O
    sugar-free strawberry
    gelatin

Preheat oven to 350 degrees. Spray a 9-by-9-inch cake pan with butter-flavored cooking spray. Sprinkle marshmallows in prepared cake pan. In a large bowl, combine flour, dry pudding mix, Splenda, baking powder, and baking soda. In a small bowl, combine yogurt and dry milk powder. Add egg, water, and vanilla extract. Mix well to combine. Add yogurt mixture to flour mixture, mixing until well combined. Pour batter evenly over marshmallows. In a medium bowl, combine undrained strawberries and dry gelatin. Spoon mixture evenly over batter. Bake for 25 to 35 minutes. Place cake pan on a wire rack and allow to cool. Cut into 8 servings.

Each serving equals:

DIABETIC EXCHANGES: 2 Starch/Carbohydrate

153 Calories • 1 gm Fat • 6 gm Protein •
30 gm Carbohydrate • 513 mg Sodium •
156 mg Calcium • 1 gm Fiber

HE: 1 Bread • ¼ Fat Free Milk • ¼ Fruit • ¼ Slider •
17 Optional Calories

Bananas Foster Upside-Down Cake

I seem to recall glamorous people in '40s movies ordering Bananas Foster when dining at some fancy restaurant, but you don't have to live in a skyscraper to adore this jazzy dessert! I decided to couple it with that classic '50s treat, the upside-down cake, for a real "blast from the past"! ☻ Serves 8

1 tablespoon + 1 teaspoon
   I Can't Believe Its Not
   Butter! Light margarine,
   melted
¾ cup Splenda Granular ☆
1 teaspoon rum extract
2 cups (2 medium) sliced
   bananas
1½ cups all-purpose flour
½ teaspoon baking soda

¼ cup chopped pecans
¾ cup plain fat-free yogurt
⅓ cup Carnation Nonfat Dry
   Milk Powder
½ cup unsweetened
   applesauce
2 eggs, slightly beaten, or
   equivalent in
   egg substitute
1 teaspoon vanilla extract

Preheat oven to 350 degrees. Spray an 8-by-8-inch baking dish with butter-flavored cooking spray. In a medium bowl, combine margarine, ¼ cup Splenda, and rum extract. Blend in bananas. Sprinkle mixture evenly into prepared baking dish. In a medium bowl, combine flour, baking soda, remaining ½ cup Splenda, and pecans. In a small bowl, combine yogurt and dry milk powder. Stir in applesauce, eggs, and vanilla extract. Add to flour mixture. Stir until smooth. Pour batter evenly over banana mixture. Bake for 35 to 40 minutes or until a toothpick inserted in center comes out clean. Place baking dish on a wire rack and cool for 10 minutes. Loosen side with knife. Place a serving plate upside down over pan and invert cake onto plate. Cut into 8 servings.

Each serving equals:

DIABETIC EXCHANGES: 1 Starch/Carbohydrate • 1 Fat •
1 Fruit

192 Calories • 4 gm Fat • 7 gm Protein •
32 gm Carbohydrate • 203 mg Sodium •
91 mg Calcium • 2 gm Fiber

HE: 1 Bread • ¾ Fat • ⅔ Fruit • ¼ Fat Free Milk •
¼ Protein • 9 Optional Calories

Pineapple Dump Cake

My grandbabies have always loved pineapple, so I like coming up with new ways to make them smile those beautiful smiles! This cake looks extra festive with its topping of coconut and pecans, so you can feel confident bringing it to the office for a birthday party or a summer picnic by the lake. The boys give it ten Yum-Yums!

🙂 Serves 8

1½ cups all-purpose flour
1½ teaspoons baking soda
1 (4-serving) package JELL-O sugar-free instant vanilla pudding mix
½ cup + 2 tablespoons Splenda Granular ☆
1 (8-ounce) can crushed pineapple, packed in fruit juice, undrained
¾ cup plain fat-free yogurt

⅓ cup Carnation Nonfat Dry Milk Powder
1 teaspoon vanilla extract
1 (8-ounce) package Philadelphia fat-free cream cheese
1 teaspoon coconut extract
½ cup Cool Whip Free
2 tablespoons flaked coconut
2 tablespoons chopped pecans

Preheat oven to 350 degrees. Spray a 9-by-9-inch cake pan with butter-flavored cooking spray. In a large bowl, combine flour, baking soda, dry pudding mix, and ½ cup Splenda. Add undrained pineapple, yogurt, dry milk powder, and vanilla extract. Mix well to combine. Pour mixture into prepared cake pan. Bake for 30 to 40 minutes or until a toothpick inserted in center comes out clean. Place cake pan on a wire rack and cool completely. In a medium bowl, stir cream cheese with a spoon until soft. Stir in remaining 2 tablespoons Splenda, coconut extract, and Cool Whip Free. Spread mixture evenly over cooled cake. Evenly sprinkle coconut and pecans over top. Cut into 8 servings. Refrigerate leftovers.

Each serving equals:

DIABETIC EXCHANGES: 2 Starch/Carbohydrate • ½ Meat

186 Calories • 2 gm Fat • 9 gm Protein •
33 gm Carbohydrate • 608 mg Sodium •
86 mg Calcium • 1 gm Fiber

HE: 1 Bread • ½ Protein • ¼ Fruit •
¼ Fat Free Milk • ¼ Fat • ¼ Slider •
10 Optional Calories

Frosted Pumpkin Cake

Were you the kind of kid who hung around the kitchen when someone (Mom? Grandma?) was baking and begged to lick the icing bowl? Join the club! Ever since childhood, I've loved desserts that come with frosting, so I knew this cake needed a sweet and creamy topping to finish it up just right. ☻ Serves 6

1 (8-ounce) can crushed pineapple, packed in fruit juice, drained, and liquid reserved

1 (15-ounce) can solid-packed pumpkin

2 eggs or equivalent in egg substitute

2 teaspoons vanilla extract ☆

1⅓ cups Carnation Nonfat Dry Milk Powder

¾ cup all-purpose flour

2 teaspoons pumpkin pie spice

½ teaspoon baking soda

½ cup + 2 tablespoons Splenda Granular ☆

½ cup raisins

1 (8-ounce) package Philadelphia fat-free cream cheese

½ cup Cool Whip Free

2 tablespoons chopped pecans

Preheat oven to 350 degrees. Spray a 9-by-9-inch cake pan with butter-flavored cooking spray. Add enough water to reserved pineapple juice to make ⅓ cup liquid. In a medium bowl, combine liquid, pumpkin, eggs, and 1 teaspoon vanilla extract. Add dry milk powder, flour, pumpkin pie spice, baking soda, and ½ cup Splenda. Mix well to combine. Stir in raisins. Spread mixture evenly into prepared cake pan. Bake for 30 minutes. Place cake pan on a wire rack and allow to cool. In a small bowl, stir cream cheese with a spoon until soft. Add remaining 2 tablespoons Splenda, remaining 1 teaspoon vanilla extract, and pineapple. Fold in Cool Whip Free. Spread mixture evenly over cooled cake. Sprinkle pecans evenly over top. Cut into 6 servings. Refrigerate leftovers.

Each serving equals:

DIABETIC EXCHANGES: 1½ Starch/Carbohydrate •
1 Meat • 1 Fruit • ½ Fat

---

292 Calories • 4 gm Fat • 16 gm Protein •
48 gm Carbohydrate • 445 mg Sodium •
234 mg Calcium • 4 gm Fiber

HE: 1 Protein • 1 Fruit • ⅔ Bread • ⅔ Vegetable •
⅔ Fat Free Milk • ⅓ Fat • ⅓ Protein • ¼ Slider

Zucchini Cake with Orange Marmalade Frosting

Even if you've never LOVED zucchini, the vegetable, you'll soon adore zucchini, the secret baking ingredient that will make your cake so moist you'll stand up and cheer! This is so rich and flavorful, you'll be tempted to plant a bigger zucchini patch next year!

◖ Serves 8

1 cup + 2 tablespoons all-purpose flour
1 cup bran flakes
1 teaspoon baking powder
½ teaspoon baking soda
1 teaspoon pumpkin pie spice
½ cup Splenda Granular
1 cup shredded unpeeled zucchini
6 tablespoons raisins
¼ cup chopped walnuts

½ cup unsweetened applesauce
½ cup fat-free milk
1 egg or equivalent in egg substitute
1 teaspoon vanilla extract
1 (8-ounce) package Philadelphia fat-free cream cheese
¼ cup orange marmalade spreadable fruit
½ cup Cool Whip Free

Preheat oven to 350 degrees. Spray a 9-by-9-inch cake pan with butter-flavored cooking spray. In a large bowl, combine flour, bran flakes, baking powder, baking soda, pumpkin pie spice, and Splenda. Stir in zucchini, raisins, and walnuts. In a small bowl, combine applesauce, milk, and egg. Stir in vanilla extract. Add applesauce mixture to flour mixture. Mix gently just to combine. Spread mixture evenly into prepared cake pan. Bake for 30 to 35 minutes or until a toothpick inserted in center comes out clean. Place cake pan on a wire rack and allow to cool. In a medium bowl, stir cream cheese with a spoon until soft. Add spreadable fruit and Cool Whip Free. Mix gently to combine. Spread mixture evenly over cooled cake. Cut into 8 servings. Refrigerate leftovers.

Each serving equals:

DIABETIC EXCHANGES: 1 Starch/Carbohydrate •
1 Fruit • ½ Meat • ½ Fat

---

195 Calories • 3 gm Fat • 8 gm Protein •
34 gm Carbohydrate • 365 mg Sodium •
64 mg Calcium • 2 gm Fiber

HE: 1 Bread • 1 Fruit • ¾ Protein • ¼ Vegetable •
¼ Fat • 19 Optional Calories

Chocolate Raspberry Cake

Remember that old commercial that told you to double your pleasure and double your fun? That must have been the tune I was humming when I stirred fresh raspberries *and* raspberry spreadable fruit into this delectable cake! ☻ Serves 8

1½ cups all-purpose flour
¼ cup unsweetened cocoa
¾ cup Splenda Granular
1 teaspoon baking powder
½ teaspoon baking soda
¼ cup chopped slivered
   almonds ☆
½ cup plain fat-free yogurt

⅓ cup Kraft fat-free
   mayonnaise
¾ cup water
2 teaspoons almond extract ☆
6 tablespoons raspberry
   spreadable fruit
1 cup Cool Whip Free
1½ cups fresh raspberries ☆

Preheat oven to 350 degrees. Spray a 9-by-9-inch cake pan with butter-flavored cooking spray. In a large bowl, combine flour, cocoa, Splenda, baking powder, and baking soda. Stir in 2 tablespoons almonds. In a small bowl, combine yogurt, mayonnaise, water, and 1 teaspoon almond extract. Add yogurt mixture to flour mixture. Mix gently to combine. Spread batter into prepared cake pan. Bake for 30 minutes or until a toothpick inserted in center comes out clean. Place cake pan on a wire rack and allow to cool completely. In a large bowl, stir spreadable fruit with a spoon until soft. Stir in Cool Whip Free and remaining 1 teaspoon almond extract. Reserve 8 raspberries. Gently fold remaining raspberries into whipped topping mixture. Frost cooled cake with raspberry mixture. Sprinkle remaining 2 tablespoons almonds over top. Evenly garnish with reserved raspberries. Cut into 8 servings. Refrigerate leftovers.

Each serving equals:

DIABETIC EXCHANGES: 1½ Starch/Carbohydrate •
1 Fruit • ½ Fat

186 Calories • 2 gm Fat • 5 gm Protein •
37 gm Carbohydrate • 321 mg Sodium •
85 mg Calcium • 3 gm Fiber

HE: 1 Bread • 1 Fruit • ¼ Fat • ½ Slider •
8 Optional Calories

Chocolate Buster Cake with Peanut Butter Frosting

Have you always considered peanut butter off-limits because of its high fat content? Many people do, but now that we've got reduced-fat versions to choose from, we can enjoy this beloved flavor without fear. And just a little bit goes a long way toward convincing you that you're in PB Heaven. The frosting of this rich cake is a good example of that! ☻ Serves 8

1½ cups all-purpose flour
¾ cup Splenda Granular
¼ cup unsweetened cocoa
1 teaspoon baking powder
½ teaspoon baking soda
¼ cup chopped dry-roasted
    peanuts ☆
½ cup plain fat-free yogurt
⅓ cup Kraft fat-free
    mayonnaise

1½ cups water ☆
1 teaspoon vanilla extract
1 (4-serving) package JELL-O
    sugar-free instant vanilla
    pudding mix
⅔ cup Carnation Nonfat Dry
    Milk Powder
¼ cup Peter Pan reduced-fat
    peanut butter
½ cup Cool Whip Free

Preheat oven to 350 degrees. Spray a 9-by-9-inch cake pan with butter-flavored cooking spray. In a large bowl, combine flour, Splenda, cocoa, baking powder, and baking soda. Stir in 3 tablespoons peanuts. In a medium bowl, combine yogurt, mayonnaise, ½ cup water, and vanilla extract. Mix well until blended. Add yogurt mixture to flour mixture. Mix gently just until combined. Spread mixture evenly into prepared cake pan. Bake for 25 to 30 minutes or until a toothpick inserted in center comes out clean. Place cake pan on a wire rack and allow to cool completely. In a medium bowl, combine dry pudding mix, dry milk powder, and remaining 1 cup water. Mix well using a wire whisk. Blend in peanut butter. Add Cool Whip Free. Mix well to combine. Spread frosting mixture evenly over cooled cake. Sprinkle remaining 1 tablespoon peanuts over top. Cut into 8 servings. Refrigerate leftovers.

Each serving equals:

DIABETIC EXCHANGES: 1½ Starch/Carbohydrate • 1 Fat • ½ Meat

217 Calories • 5 gm Fat • 9 gm Protein • 34 gm Carbohydrate • 552 mg Sodium • 140 mg Calcium • 2 gm Fiber

HE: 1 Bread • ¾ Fat • ⅔ Protein • ⅓ Fat Free Milk • ½ Slider • 8 Optional Calories

Chocolate Cake with German Chocolate Frosting

We celebrate birthdays every single month at Healthy Exchanges, and I knew if I chose this cake for one of those monthly parties, I'd be very, very popular! The rich chocolate flavor of the cake and the frosting pleased our resident chocoholics, and the coconut and nuts on top sent everyone else into ecstasy! ☻ Serves 8

1½ cups all-purpose flour
¾ cup Splenda Granular
1 teaspoon baking powder
½ teaspoon baking soda
¼ cup unsweetened cocoa
⅓ cup plain fat-free yogurt
¼ cup Kraft fat-free mayonnaise
2 teaspoons vanilla extract ☆
2¼ cups water

1 (4-serving) package JELL-O sugar-free chocolate cook-and-serve pudding mix
⅔ cup Carnation Nonfat Dry Milk Powder
2 teaspoons coconut extract
2⅔ teaspoons I Can't Believe It's Not Butter! Light margarine
¼ cup chopped pecans
¼ cup flaked coconut

Preheat oven to 350 degrees. Spray a 9-by-9-inch cake pan with butter-flavored cooking spray. In a large bowl, combine flour, Splenda, baking powder, baking soda, and cocoa. In a small bowl, combine yogurt, mayonnaise, 1 teaspoon vanilla extract, and 1 cup water. Add yogurt mixture to flour mixture. Mix well to combine. Spread batter into prepared cake pan. Bake for 30 to 35 minutes or until a toothpick inserted in center comes out clean. Place cake pan on a wire rack and allow to cool. Meanwhile, in a medium saucepan, combine dry pudding mix, dry milk powder, and remaining 1¼ cups water. Cook over medium heat until mixture thickens and starts to boil, stirring often. Remove from heat. Stir in remaining 1 teaspoon vanilla extract, coconut extract, and margarine. Add pecans and coconut. Mix well to combine. Spread hot mixture evenly over partially cooled cake. Allow frosted cake to cool completely. Cut into 8 servings.

Each serving equals:

DIABETIC EXCHANGES: 1½ Starch/Carbohydrate • 1 Fruit • ½ Fat

180 Calories • 4 gm Fat • 6 gm Protein • 30 gm Carbohydrate • 311 mg Sodium • 130 mg Calcium • 2 gm Fiber

HE: 1 Bread • ⅔ Fat • ¼ Fat Free Milk • ½ Slider • 3 Optional Calories

Mocha Raisin Cake

One of the real challenges in baking healthy cakes is keeping them moist. This recipe employs fat-free mayonnaise and fat-free yogurt to perform this particular magic, and I'm certain you'll be pleased at the sweet and tender result. You may want to try this cake with several kinds of coffee, especially if you're into drinking the exotic flavored blends. ☕ Serves 8

1½ cups all-purpose flour
¼ cup unsweetened cocoa
¾ cup Splenda Granular
1 teaspoon baking powder
½ teaspoon baking soda
1½ teaspoons instant coffee
    crystals ☆
¾ cup raisins ☆
⅓ cup Kraft fat-free
    mayonnaise

⅓ cup plain fat-free yogurt
2 cups water ☆
1 teaspoon vanilla extract
1 (4-serving) package JELL-O
    sugar-free instant
    chocolate pudding mix
⅔ cup Carnation Nonfat Dry
    Milk Powder
¾ cup Cool Whip Lite

Preheat oven to 350 degrees. Spray a 9-by-9-inch cake pan with butter-flavored cooking spray. In a large bowl, combine flour, cocoa, Splenda, baking powder, baking soda, and 1 teaspoon coffee. Reserve 2 tablespoons raisins. Stir in remaining raisins. Add mayonnaise, yogurt, 1 cup water, and vanilla extract. Mix gently to combine. Spread batter into prepared cake pan. Bake 30 to 35 minutes or until a toothpick inserted in center comes out clean. Place cake pan on a wire rack and allow to cool completely. In a medium bowl, combine dry pudding mix, dry milk powder, remaining ½ teaspoon coffee crystals, and remaining 1 cup water. Mix well using a wire whisk. Blend in Cool Whip Lite. Spread topping mixture evenly over cake. Evenly sprinkle remaining 2 tablespoons raisins over top. Cut into 8 servings. Refrigerate leftovers.

Each serving equals:

DIABETIC EXCHANGES: 1½ Starch/Carbohydrate •
1 Fruit

197 Calories • 1 gm Fat • 6 gm Protein •
41 gm Carbohydrate • 510 mg Sodium •
135 mg Calcium • 2 gm Fiber

HE: 1 Bread • ¾ Fruit • ¼ Fat Free Milk • ½ Slider •
6 Optional Calories

Pear-Gingerbread Cake

Gingerbread is such wonderfully old-fashioned comfort food, yet many people have never tried to make it at home. This beautifully nutty and fruity dessert will bring back great memories—and create some new ones! ☻ Serves 8

1½ cups all-purpose flour
2 tablespoons Splenda
    Granular
2 teaspoons baking powder
1 teaspoon ground ginger
1 (4-serving) package JELL-O
    sugar-free instant vanilla
    pudding mix
6 tablespoons raisins

¼ cup chopped walnuts
½ cup fat-free milk
1 egg or equivalent in egg
    substitute
½ cup unsweetened applesauce
1 (16-ounce) can pear halves,
    packed in fruit juice,
    drained, and coarsely
    chopped

Preheat oven to 375 degrees. Spray a 9-by-9-inch cake pan with butter-flavored cooking spray. In a large bowl, combine flour, Splenda, baking powder, ginger, and dry pudding mix. Stir in raisins and walnuts. In a small bowl, combine milk, egg, and applesauce. Add milk mixture to flour mixture. Mix well to combine. Fold in pears. Evenly spread batter into prepared cake pan. Bake for 25 to 30 minutes or until a toothpick inserted in center comes out clean. Place cake pan on a wire rack and cool completely. Cut into 8 servings.

HINT: Good served with 1 tablespoon Cool Whip Lite. If using, don't forget to count the few additional calories.

Each serving equals:

DIABETIC EXCHANGES: 1½ Starch • 1 Fruit

203 Calories • 3 gm Fat • 4 gm Protein •
40 gm Carbohydrate • 308 mg Sodium •
104 mg Calcium • 3 gm Fiber

HE: 1 Bread • 1 Fruit • ¼ Protein • ¼ Fat •
19 Optional Calories

Super Shortcakes

and Colossal

Cobblers

My first love in food is, and has always been, strawberries. When I was young, I used to get sore throats and croup every time the seasons changed. Daddy always went to the store and got me frozen strawberries to soothe my aching throat. This was especially wonderful during those times of the year—fall, winter, and spring—when fresh strawberries were impossible to find back in the '50s.

I know I connect my love of strawberries, and strawberry shortcake, with my love of my mother's cooking and my memory of my father's love. Every time I eat those strawberries, I think of Daddy going up to the store in any weather to make his daughter feel better.

I also recall with sweet pleasure my grandmother's wonderful way with fruit cobblers, cozy and warm and bubbling over with ripe, gorgeous fruit. They take so little time to prepare, but they show so much love!

I still need what I had when I was younger, those great memories and delicious desserts, but now I need them in a healthy way. So I keep inventing healthy shortcakes and cobbler recipes that recall those sweet times in my life.

Anyone who's heard me talk about desserts knows that one of the few dessert treats I'll consider ordering in a restaurant is strawberry shortcake. And when there's so much ripe, beautiful fruit available in our markets and at the farm stands, I begin imagining all the ways I might serve it: *Apple Blueberry Crisp*, or *Banana Split Shortcakes*, or maybe *Grandma's Peach Cobbler!*

Celebrate the seasons and satisfy your taste for something sweet with the recipes in this section. Cobblers and shortcakes are scrumptious, classic, old-fashioned desserts in the very best meaning of the words.

Peach Praline Shortcake

Peaches at their ripest are a great choice for shortcakes and, when combined with my favorite nuts, deliver a tummy-pleasing sensation almost as much fun as a trip to the Big Easy. If you can't make it to "Praline Central," turn your kitchen into a little bit of New Orleans with this one.　　❂　Serves 4

> 2 cups (4 medium) peeled and sliced fresh peaches ☆
> ¼ cup Splenda Granular
> ¾ cup Bisquick Reduced-Fat Baking Mix
> ¼ cup water
> 2 tablespoons Kraft fat-free mayonnaise
> 2 tablespoons chopped pecans
> ¼ cup Cool Whip Lite

Preheat oven to 425 degrees. Spray a baking sheet with butter-flavored cooking spray. Place 1 cup peaches in a blender container. Cover and process on HIGH until mixture is smooth. Pour mixture into a medium bowl. Stir in Splenda, and remaining 1 cup peach slices. Cover and refrigerate. In a medium bowl, combine baking mix, water, and mayonnaise. Stir in pecans. Drop by spoonfuls onto prepared baking sheet to form 4 shortcakes. Bake for 10 to 12 minutes or until golden brown. For each serving, place 1 shortcake in a dessert dish, spoon ¼ cup peach mixture over shortcake, and top with 1 tablespoon Cool Whip Lite.

Each serving equals:

DIABETIC EXCHANGES: 1 Starch/Carbohydrate •
1 Fruit • 1 Fat

200 Calories • 4 gm Fat • 3 gm Protein •
38 gm Carbohydrate • 326 mg Sodium •
28 mg Calcium • 4 gm Fiber

HE: 1 Bread • 1 Fruit • ½ Fat • ¼ Slider •
4 Optional Calories

Cornbread Shortcakes with Hot Strawberry Sauce

And now for something entirely different, and yet delightfully good. Making shortcakes with cornmeal may never have occurred to you, but it works really well, especially when they're topped with this luscious strawberry sauce!   ☻   Serves 8

½ cup + 2 tablespoons yellow cornmeal

½ cup + 1 tablespoon all-purpose flour

1½ teaspoons baking powder

¼ cup Splenda Granular

1 cup unsweetened applesauce

1 egg or equivalent in egg substitute

1 (4-serving) package JELL-O sugar-free strawberry gelatin

1 (4-serving) package JELL-O sugar-free vanilla cook-and-serve pudding mix

1¼ cups water

2 cups frozen unsweetened strawberries, thawed, drained, and ¼ cup liquid reserved

Preheat oven to 350 degrees. Spray 8 wells of a 12-hole muffin pan with butter-flavored cooking spray. In a large bowl, combine cornmeal, flour, baking powder, and Splenda. In a small bowl, combine applesauce and egg. Add applesauce mixture to cornmeal mixture. Mix well to combine. Evenly spoon batter into prepared muffin wells. Bake for 25 to 30 minutes or until a toothpick inserted in center comes out clean. Meanwhile in a medium saucepan, combine dry gelatin, dry pudding mix, water, and reserved strawberry liquid. Cook over medium heat until mixture thickens and starts to boil, stirring constantly. Stir in strawberries. Lower heat, and simmer until muffins are done, stirring occasionally. For each serving, place 1 muffin in a dessert dish and spoon about ¼ cup strawberry mixture over top. Also good served cold.

HINTS: 1. Fill unused muffin wells with water. It protects the muffin pan and ensures even baking.
2. Reheat leftover sauce in microwave before serving.

Each serving equals:

DIABETIC EXCHANGES: 1 Starch • ½ Fruit

121 Calories • 1 gm Fat • 4 gm Protein •
24 gm Carbohydrate • 185 mg Sodium •
62 mg Calcium • 2 gm Fiber

HE: 1 Bread • ½ Fruit • ¼ Slider • 6 Optional Calories

Mocha Shortcakes with Strawberry Sauce

This one's for all you chocolate and coffee fans out there (and I know there are many of you)! Mocha is one of America's favorite flavors, so I decided to transform the classic shortcake into mocha magic. Choose the ripest, sweetest berries you can find to top this off!

○ Serves 4

4 cups sliced fresh
    strawberries ☆
¾ cup Splenda Granular ☆
¾ cup Bisquick Reduced-Fat
    Baking Mix
⅓ cup Carnation Nonfat Dry
    Milk Powder
¼ cup Nesquick sugar-free
    chocolate drink mix

1 teaspoon instant coffee
    crystals
¼ cup Kraft fat-free
    mayonnaise
¼ cup water
1 teaspoon vanilla extract
¼ cup Cool Whip Lite

Preheat oven to 375 degrees. Spray 4 wells of a muffin pan with butter-flavored cooking spray. Place 1½ cups strawberries in a large bowl. Mash with potato masher or a fork. Stir in ½ cup Splenda. Add remaining 2½ cups strawberries. Mix gently to combine. Cover and refrigerate. Meanwhile, in a medium bowl, combine baking mix, dry milk powder, chocolate mix, coffee crystals, and remaining ¼ cup Splenda. Add mayonnaise, water, and vanilla extract. Mix well to combine. Evenly spoon batter into prepared muffin wells. Bake for 15 to 20 minutes or until a toothpick inserted in center comes out clean. Place muffin pan on a wire rack and allow to cool for 5 minutes. Remove muffins from pan and cool completely on wire rack. For each serving, split shortcake in half, place bottom half on a serving plate, spoon about ½ cup strawberry mixture over top, arrange top half over strawberries, spoon about ½ cup strawberry mixture over top, and garnish with 1 tablespoon Cool Whip Lite.

HINT: Fill unused muffin wells with water. It protects the muffin
pan and ensures even baking.

Each serving equals:

DIABETIC EXCHANGES: 2 Starch/Carbohydrate • 1 Fruit

223 Calories • 3 gm Fat • 5 gm Protein •
44 gm Carbohydrate • 451 mg Sodium •
113 mg Calcium • 3 gm Fiber

HE: 1 Bread • 1 Fruit • ¼ Fat Free Milk • ½ Slider •
8 Optional Calories

Orange Strawberry Shortcakes

This looks so bright and pretty, it's a great choice to serve on one of those gray, rainy days you sometimes get even in the middle of a hot Iowa summer! There's just something so energizing about orange and strawberry together, and don't forget you're also getting a nice "shot" of vitamin C! ☻ Serves 4

2 cups sliced fresh strawberries ☆
½ cup Splenda Granular ☆
1 (11-ounce) can mandarin oranges, rinsed and drained
¾ cup Bisquick Reduced-Fat Baking Mix
⅓ cup Carnation Nonfat Dry Milk Powder
2 tablespoons chopped pecans
¼ cup Kraft fat-free mayonnaise
½ cup unsweetened orange juice
1 teaspoon coconut extract
¼ cup Cool Whip Lite
1 tablespoon + 1 teaspoon flaked coconut

Preheat oven to 375 degrees. Spray a baking sheet with butter-flavored cooking spray. Place ½ cup strawberries in a medium bowl. Mash with a potato masher or a fork. Stir in ¼ cup Splenda. Add remaining 1½ cups strawberries and mandarin oranges. Mix well to combine. Cover and refrigerate. In a medium bowl, combine baking mix, remaining ¼ cup Splenda, dry milk powder, and pecans. Add mayonnaise, orange juice, and coconut extract. Mix well to combine. Drop by large spoonfuls onto prepared baking sheet to form 4 shortcakes. Bake for 15 to 20 minutes. Place baking sheet on a wire rack and allow shortcakes to cool for 10 minutes. For each serving, place 1 shortcake in a dessert dish, spoon about ½ cup strawberry mixture over top, and garnish with 1 tablespoon Cool Whip Lite and 1 teaspoon coconut.

Each serving equals:

DIABETIC EXCHANGES: 1½ Starch/Carbohydrate •
1 Fruit • 1 Fat

217 Calories • 5 gm Fat • 5 gm Protein •
38 gm Carbohydrate • 431 mg Sodium •
108 mg Calcium • 2 gm Fiber

HE: 1¼ Fruit • 1 Bread • ½ Fat • ¼ Fat Free Milk •
¼ Slider • 17 Optional Calories

Banana Split Shortcakes

This is a wonderful treat for special occasions yet it's so easy, you can stir it up anytime you wish! ☻ Serves 6

1 (4-serving) package JELL-O
    sugar-free vanilla cook-
    and-serve pudding mix
1 (8-ounce) can crushed
    pineapple, packed in
    fruit juice, undrained
1¼ cups water ☆
1 cup (1 medium) sliced
    banana
2 cups sliced fresh strawberries
3 tablespoons Splenda
    Granular

1 cup + 2 tablespoons Bisquick
    Reduced-Fat Baking Mix
⅔ cup Carnation Nonfat Dry
    Milk Powder
3 tablespoons Kraft fat-free
    mayonnaise
1 teaspoon vanilla extract
3 cups Wells' Blue Bunny
    sugar- and fat-free vanilla
    ice cream or any sugar-
    and fat-free ice cream
6 tablespoons Cool Whip Lite

Preheat oven to 415 degrees. Spray 6 wells of a muffin pan with butter-flavored cooking spray. In a medium saucepan, combine dry pudding mix, undrained pineapple, and ¾ cup water. Mix well. Cook over medium heat until mixture thickens and starts to boil, stirring constantly. Remove from heat. Stir in banana and strawberries. Place saucepan on a wire rack and allow to cool. Meanwhile in a medium bowl, combine Splenda, baking mix, and dry milk powder. Add mayonnaise, remaining ½ cup water, and vanilla extract. Mix well to combine. Evenly fill prepared muffin wells. Bake for 8 to 10 minutes or until golden brown. For each serving, split shortcake in half, place bottom half in a dessert dish, top with ½ cup ice cream, arrange top half of shortcake over ice cream, spoon about ½ cup fruit mixture over top, and garnish with 1 tablespoon Cool Whip Lite.

HINT: Fill unused muffin wells with water. It protects the muffin
       pan and ensures even baking.

Each serving equals:

DIABETIC EXCHANGES: 2 Starch/Carbohydrate • 1 Fruit

242 Calories • 2 gm Fat • 9 gm Protein •
47 gm Carbohydrate • 495 mg Sodium •
244 mg Calcium • 2 gm Fiber

HE: 1 Bread • 1 Fruit • ¼ Fat Free Milk • 1 Slider •
11 Optional Calories

Fruit Cocktail Shortcake

Here's what I call a perfect pantry shortcake recipe—the ingredients are probably sitting on your shelves right now, it can be prepared in only minutes, and it's bound to please dessert lovers from 2 to 92!

◐ Serves 4

> ¾ cup Bisquick Reduced-Fat Baking Mix
> 1 cup Carnation Nonfat Dry Milk Powder ☆
> ¼ cup pourable Splenda Granular
> ¼ cup Kraft fat-free mayonnaise
> 1¾ cups water ☆
> 1 teaspoon vanilla extract
> 1 (4-serving) package JELL-O sugar-free instant vanilla
>   pudding mix
> 1 (16-ounce) can fruit cocktail, packed in fruit juice,
>   drained, and ½ cup liquid reserved
> ¼ cup Cool Whip Lite

Preheat oven to 415 degrees. Spray a baking sheet with butter-flavored cooking spray. In a medium bowl, combine baking mix, ⅓ cup dry milk powder, and Splenda. Add mayonnaise, ½ cup water, and vanilla extract. Mix well to combine. Drop by spoonfuls onto prepared baking sheet to form 4 shortcakes. Bake for 8 to 12 minutes or until golden brown. Place baking sheet on a wire rack and allow to cool. Meanwhile, in a medium bowl, combine dry pudding mix and remaining ⅔ cup dry milk powder. Add reserved fruit cocktail liquid and remaining 1¼ cups water. Mix well using a wire whisk. Blend in fruit cocktail. For each serving, place 1 shortcake in a dessert dish, spoon about ¼ cup pudding mixture over shortcake, and top with 1 tablespoon Cool Whip Lite. Serve at once or refrigerate until ready to serve.

Each serving equals:

DIABETIC EXCHANGES: 1 Starch/Carbohydrate •
1 Fruit • 1 Fat Free Milk

---

242 Calories • 2 gm Fat • 8 gm Protein •
48 gm Carbohydrate • 755 mg Sodium •
237 mg Calcium • 2 gm Fiber

HE: 1 Bread • 1 Fruit • ¾ Fat Free Milk • ½ Slider •
17 Optional Calories

Warm Peach Melba Shortcakes

My mouth was practically watering as I was writing down this recipe, imagining how luscious a warm and peachy topping would taste over a classic shortcake. ☻ Serves 4

¾ cup Bisquick Reduced-Fat Baking Mix
⅓ cup Carnation Nonfat Dry Milk Powder
2 tablespoons Splenda Granular
2 tablespoons Kraft fat-free mayonnaise
⅓ cup water
1 (4-serving) package JELL-O sugar-free vanilla cook-and-serve
    pudding mix
1 (4-serving) package JELL-O sugar-free raspberry gelatin
1 (8-ounce) can sliced peaches, packed in fruit juice, drained, and
    ¼ cup liquid reserved
1¼ cups warm water
1½ cups frozen unsweetened raspberries
¼ cup Cool Whip Lite

Preheat oven to 415 degrees. Spray a baking sheet with butter-flavored cooking spray. In a medium bowl, combine baking mix, dry milk powder, and Splenda. Add mayonnaise and ⅓ cup water. Mix well to combine. Drop by tablespoonfuls onto prepared baking sheet to form 4 shortcakes. Bake for 8 to 12 minutes or until golden brown. Place baking sheet on a wire rack and allow shortcakes to cool. In a medium saucepan, combine dry pudding mix, dry gelatin, reserved peach liquid, and 1¼ cups water. Cook over medium heat until mixture thickens and starts to boil, stirring often. Gently stir in frozen raspberries. Continue cooking until raspberries start to thaw. Add peaches. Mix gently to combine. Remove from heat. Place saucepan on a wire rack and allow to cool. For each serving, place shortcake in a dessert dish, spoon ¾ cup sauce over top, and garnish with 1 tablespoon Cool Whip Lite.

Each serving equals:

DIABETIC EXCHANGES: 2 Starch/Carbohydrate • 1 Fruit

198 Calories • 2 gm Fat • 6 gm Protein •
39 gm Carbohydrate • 529 mg Sodium •
101 mg Calcium • 3 gm Fiber

HE: 1 Bread • 1 Fruit • ¼ Fat Free Milk • ½ Slider •
13 Optional Calories

Cherry Shortcakes

Thank heaven that canned cherries retain so much sweet satisfaction, because fresh cherries tend to be quite expensive and have a very short season! If you enjoy cherries as much as our country's first president did, then this is a great way to serve them!

☻ Serves 4

> 1 (16-ounce) can tart red cherries, packed in water, undrained
>
> ³⁄₄ cup water
>
> 1 (4-serving) package JELL-O sugar-free vanilla cook-and-serve pudding mix
>
> 1 (4-serving) package JELL-O sugar-free cherry gelatin
>
> ½ teaspoon almond extract
>
> ³⁄₄ cup Bisquick Reduced-Fat Baking Mix
>
> ½ cup Splenda Granular
>
> ½ cup water
>
> ¼ cup Kraft fat-free mayonnaise
>
> ¼ cup Cool Whip Lite
>
> 1 tablespoon + 1 teaspoon chopped almonds

Preheat oven to 375 degrees. Spray a baking sheet with butter-flavored cooking spray. In a medium saucepan, combine undrained cherries, water, dry pudding mix, and dry gelatin. Cook over medium heat until mixture thickens and starts to boil, stirring constantly. Remove from heat. Stir in almond extract. Place saucepan on a wire rack and cool while preparing shortcakes. In a large bowl, combine baking mix, Splenda, water, and mayonnaise. Drop batter by large spoonfuls onto prepared baking sheet to form 4 shortcakes. Bake for 10 to 15 minutes or until golden brown. For each serving, place 1 shortcake in a dessert dish, spoon ½ cup cherry mixture over shortcake, top with 1 tablespoon Cool Whip Lite, and garnish with 1 teaspoon almonds.

Each serving equals:

DIABETIC EXCHANGES: 1½ Starch/Carbohydrate •
1 Fruit • ½ Fat

191 Calories • 3 gm Fat • 4 gm Protein •
37 gm Carbohydrate • 569 mg Sodium •
39 mg Calcium • 1 gm Fiber

HE: 1 Bread • 1 Fruit • ¾ Slider •
10 Optional Calories

Easy Apple Pecan Crisp

While this was baking away in the kitchen, our employees kept peeking in during their breaks to ask what the *amazing* aroma was! The power of old-fashioned spices to bring back our best cozy memories is sometimes quite astonishing. If you want your house to be as welcoming as it can be, put a dish of this in the oven to bake just before your guests arrive! ☻ Serves 6

1 (4-serving) package JELL-O sugar-free vanilla cook-and-serve pudding mix
1 cup unsweetened apple juice
½ cup water
1 teaspoon apple pie spice
2 cups (6 small) cored, unpeeled, and chopped cooking apples

½ cup + 1 tablespoon Bisquick Reduced-Fat Baking Mix
¼ cup Splenda Granular
3 tablespoons chopped pecans
3 tablespoons Land O Lakes no-fat sour cream

Preheat oven to 350 degrees. Spray an 8-by-8-inch baking dish with butter-flavored cooking spray. In a large saucepan, combine dry pudding mix, apple juice, water, and apple pie spice. Stir in apples. Cook over medium heat until mixture thickens and apples become soft, stirring often. Spoon apple mixture into prepared baking dish. In a large bowl, combine baking mix, Splenda, and pecans. Add sour cream. Mix well with a fork until blended and crumbly. Sprinkle topping mixture evenly over apples. Bake for 30 minutes or until top is browned and filling is bubbly. Divide into 6 servings.

Each serving equals:

DIABETIC EXCHANGES: 1 Fruit • ½ Starch • ½ Fat

127 Calories • 3 gm Fat • 1 gm Protein •
24 gm Carbohydrate • 219 mg Sodium •
24 mg Calcium • 1 gm Fiber

HE: 1 Fruit • ½ Bread • ½ Fat • ¼ Slider •
3 Optional Calories

Apple Blueberry Crisp

It can be confusing when you're standing in the market trying to choose the right products for your healthy lifestyle. There are just so many choices. Applesauce is a perfect example of this, so be sure to read the labels and select an unsweetened product. Some manufacturers call this "natural," but check to be sure no sugar has been added. Applesauce has so many great uses in healthy cooking, you should always have a jar in your fridge or pantry.   ☻   Serves 6

1 (4-serving) package JELL-O sugar-free vanilla cook-and-serve pudding mix
1 (4-serving) package JELL-O sugar-free lemon gelatin
1¼ cups water
1½ cups (3 small) cored, unpeeled, and diced cooking apples

1½ cups fresh or frozen unsweetened blueberries
6 tablespoons all-purpose flour
6 tablespoons quick oats
¼ cup Splenda Granular
½ teaspoon apple pie spice
½ cup unsweetened applesauce

Preheat oven to 350 degrees. In a medium saucepan, combine dry pudding mix, dry gelatin, and water. Mix well. Stir in apples. Cook over medium heat until mixture thickens and apples become slightly soft, stirring constantly. Remove from heat. Place saucepan on a wire rack and allow to cool for 15 minutes. Gently fold in blueberries. Pour mixture into a 9-inch pie plate. In a medium bowl, combine flour, oats, Splenda, and apple pie spice. Add applesauce. Mix well to combine. Sprinkle mixture evenly over fruit. Bake for 25 to 30 minutes or until bubbly. Cut into 6 servings.

Each serving equals:

DIABETIC EXCHANGES: 1 Fruit • ½ Starch

112 Calories • 0 gm Fat • 3 gm Protein •
25 gm Carbohydrate • 116 mg Sodium •
9 mg Calcium • 3 gm Fiber

HE: 1 Fruit • ⅔ Bread • ¼ Slider • 4 Optional Calories

Blueberry Peach Crisp

Fruit crisps are a delectable Midwestern tradition that I like to think we've sent out to the rest of the nation, and now everybody knows what a pleasure they are to prepare and to eat! This one is lovely to look at and *really* tasty. Better still, it's good with either fresh or frozen berries. ☺ Serves 6

1½ cups fresh blueberries or frozen, thawed and drained
1 (16-ounce) can sliced peaches, packed in fruit juice, drained, and ½ cup liquid reserved
¾ cup Bisquick Reduced-Fat Baking Mix
¼ cup Splenda Granular
½ teaspoon ground cinnamon
2 tablespoons I Can't Believe It's Not Butter! Light margarine
6 tablespoons Cool Whip Lite

Preheat oven to 375 degrees. Place blueberries and peaches in an 8-by-8-inch baking dish. In a medium bowl, combine baking mix, Splenda, and cinnamon. Add margarine. Mix well until mixture resembles coarse crumbs. Sprinkle mixture over fruit. Evenly drizzle reserved peach liquid over top. Bake for 25 minutes. Place baking dish on a wire rack and allow to cool slightly. Divide into 6 servings. When serving, top each with 1 tablespoon Cool Whip Lite. Good served warm or cold.

Each serving equals:

DIABETIC EXCHANGES: 1 Fruit • 1 Starch • ½ Fat

130 Calories • 2 gm Fat • 2 gm Protein •
26 gm Carbohydrate • 198 mg Sodium •
22 mg Calcium • 2 gm Fiber

HE: 1 Fruit • ¾ Bread • ½ Fat • 17 Optional Calories

Pear Raspberry Crumble

You've often heard the expression "Less is more," and it couldn't be *more* true than in this recipe. It's simple as can be, and it draws its mouthwatering flavor from the "built-in" goodness of the ingredients. Choose ripe, unblemished pears to be the heart of this delicious dessert.   ☺   Serves 8

> *3 cups (6 medium) fresh sliced pears*
> *1½ cups frozen unsweetened raspberries*
> *2 tablespoons chopped pecans*
> *½ cup Splenda Granular*
> *1 cup + 2 tablespoons Bisquick Reduced-Fat Baking Mix ☆*
> *2 tablespoons + 2 teaspoons I Can't Believe It's Not Butter! Light*
> *   margarine*

Preheat oven to 350 degrees. Spray a 9-by-9-inch cake pan with butter-flavored cooking spray. In a large bowl, combine pears, raspberries, pecans, ¼ cup Splenda, and 2 tablespoons baking mix. Spread mixture into prepared cake pan. In a medium bowl, combine remaining ¼ cup Splenda, remaining 1 cup baking mix, and margarine. Mix well with a fork until mixture is crumbly. Evenly sprinkle mixture over top. Bake for 1 hour. Place cake pan on a wire rack and allow to cool for at least 10 minutes. Cut into 8 servings. Good served warm or cold.

HINT: Also good with Cool Whip Lite or Wells' Blue Bunny sugar-
       and fat-free ice cream.

Each serving equals:

DIABETIC EXCHANGES: 1 Fruit • 1 Fat • ½ Starch

132 Calories • 4 gm Fat • 2 gm Protein •
22 gm Carbohydrate • 218 mg Sodium •
61 mg Calcium • 4 gm Fiber

HE: 1 Fruit • ¾ Bread • ¾ Fat • 6 Optional Calories

Strawberry Banana Crunch

I love the ease of "baking" in the microwave, don't you? For one thing, it keeps the number of dirty dishes low (always a plus in my book!), but even more important, it keeps whatever you're preparing really moist. If you can't find the strawberry banana gelatin, substitute strawberry—it'll still be great! ☺ Serves 6

1 (4-serving) package
   JELL-O sugar-free
   vanilla cook-and-serve
   pudding mix
1 (4-serving) package JELL-O
   sugar-free strawberry-
   banana gelatin
1 teaspoon lemon juice
¾ cup water
2 cups frozen unsweetened
   strawberries
1 cup (1 medium) sliced
   banana

¾ cup purchased graham
   cracker crumbs or
   12 (2½-inch) graham
   cracker squares made
   into crumbs
2 tablespoons Splenda
   Granular
1 tablespoon + 1 teaspoon I
   Can't Believe It's Not
   Butter! Light margarine
2 tablespoons flaked coconut
2 tablespoons chopped
   pecans

In an 8-cup glass measuring bowl, combine dry pudding mix, dry gelatin, lemon juice, and water. Microwave on HIGH (100% power) for 2 minutes. Stir in frozen strawberries. Continue microwaving on HIGH for 4 minutes, stirring after 2 minutes. Stir in banana. Pour hot mixture into an 8-by-8-inch baking dish. In a medium bowl, combine graham cracker crumbs, Splenda and margarine. Mix with a fork until mixture is crumbly. Stir in coconut and pecans. Sprinkle mixture evenly over fruit mixture. Cover and microwave on HIGH for 2 minutes. Place baking dish on a wire rack and let set at least 3 minutes. Evenly spoon mixture into 6 dessert dishes. Good hot or cold.

Each serving equals:

DIABETIC EXCHANGES: 1 Starch • 1 Fat • ½ Fruit

---

152 Calories • 4 gm Fat • 3 gm Protein •
26 gm Carbohydrate • 221 mg Sodium •
13 mg Calcium • 2 gm Fiber

HE: ⅔ Fruit • ⅔ Bread • ⅔ Fat • ¼ Slider •
12 Optional Calories

Grandma's Peach Cobbler

Even if you're far too young to be a grandmother (or you just look that way!), you'll welcome this wonderfully wholesome and old-timey dessert that makes a fantastic ice cream topping! When the kids or grandkids are stopping by, make their visit a memorable one by fixing a dish whose every bite shows how much you love them!

● Serves 6

1 (4-serving) package JELL-O
    sugar-free vanilla cook-
    and-serve pudding mix
1 (16-ounce) can peaches,
    packed in fruit juice,
    drained, and
    ⅓ cup liquid reserved

1 cup water
1 (7.5 ounce) can Pillsbury
    refrigerated buttermilk
    biscuits
¼ cup raisins
2 tablespoons Splenda Granular
½ teaspoon ground cinnamon

Preheat oven to 375 degrees. In a medium saucepan, combine dry pudding mix, peach liquid, and water. Stir in peaches. Cook over medium heat until mixture thickens and starts to boil, stirring often. Spoon hot mixture into an 8-by-8-inch baking dish. Separate biscuits and cut each into 4 pieces. Sprinkle biscuit pieces and raisins evenly over peach mixture. In a small bowl, combine Splenda and cinnamon. Evenly sprinkle mixture over top. Bake for 20 to 25 minutes or until golden brown. Place baking dish on a wire rack and let set for 5 minutes. Cut into 6 servings.

HINT: Good warm with sugar- and fat-free vanilla ice cream or cold with Cool Whip Lite.

Each serving equals:

DIABETIC EXCHANGES: 1 Starch • 1 Fruit

---

157 Calories • 1 gm Fat • 3 gm Protein •
34 gm Carbohydrate • 384 mg Sodium •
10 mg Calcium • 3 gm Fiber

HE: 1¼ Bread • 1 Fruit • 15 Optional Calories

Peach Melba Cobbler

People don't often expect a baked dessert at the height of summer, but you know as well as I do that many steamy days turn cool after the sun goes down. It's a great excuse to dazzle your guests with this luxurious cobbler just bursting with gorgeous fresh fruit!

○ Serves 6

> 1 (4-serving) package JELL-O sugar-free vanilla cook-and-serve
>   pudding mix
> 1 (4-serving) package JELL-O sugar-free raspberry gelatin
> 1 cup water
> 2 cups (4 medium) peeled and sliced fresh peaches
> 1½ cups fresh raspberries
> 1 (7.5 ounce) can Pillsbury refrigerated buttermilk biscuits
> 2 tablespoons Splenda Granular

Preheat oven to 350 degrees. Spray an 8-by-8-inch baking dish with butter-flavored cooking spray. In a large saucepan, combine dry pudding mix, dry gelatin, and water. Stir in peaches. Cook over medium heat until mixture thickens and peaches start to soften, stirring often. Remove from heat. Gently stir in raspberries. Pour fruit mixture into prepared baking dish. Separate biscuits and cut each into 4 pieces. Evenly sprinkle biscuit pieces over top of fruit mixture. Lightly spray top with butter-flavored cooking spray. Sprinkle Splenda evenly over top. Bake for 25 to 30 minutes. Place baking dish on a wire rack and let set for 5 minutes. Divide into 6 servings.

Each serving equals:

DIABETIC EXCHANGES: 1 Starch • 1 Fruit

145 Calories • 1 gm Fat • 4 gm Protein •
30 gm Carbohydrate • 417 mg Sodium •
10 mg Calcium • 4 gm Fiber

HE: 1¼ Bread • 1 Fruit • ¼ Slider •
2 Optional Calories

Fabulous Fruit Cocktail Cobbler

My kids love fruit cocktail, and so does Cliff. Some fancy gourmet cooks may look down their noses at a recipe that stars this super-market basic, but I don't care—and you won't either, once you gobble down a bite! When you're in the mood for a little variety, and you don't feel like cutting up half a dozen different fruits, it's the right choice.   ☺   Serves 4

> ¾ cup Bisquick Reduced-Fat Baking Mix
> ½ cup + 2 tablespoons Splenda Granular ☆
> ⅔ cup Carnation Nonfat Dry Milk Powder
> 2 tablespoons chopped pecans
> 1 (16-ounce) can fruit cocktail, packed in fruit juice, drained, and
>   ½ cup liquid reserved
> ½ teaspoon apple pie spice
> ½ cup Cool Whip Lite

Preheat oven to 350 degrees. Spray an 8-by-8-inch baking dish with butter-flavored cooking spray. In a large bowl, combine baking mix, ½ cup Splenda, dry milk powder, and pecans. Stir in reserved fruit cocktail liquid. Add fruit cocktail. Mix gently to combine. Spread batter into prepared baking dish. In a small bowl, combine remaining 2 tablespoons Splenda and apple pie spice. Evenly sprinkle mixture over top. Bake for 35 minutes. Place baking dish on a wire rack and let set for 5 minutes. Divide into 4 servings. Top each with 2 tablespoons Cool Whip Lite.

Each serving equals:

DIABETIC EXCHANGES: 1 Starch • 1 Fruit • ½ Fat Free Milk • ½ Fat

220 Calories • 4 gm Fat • 6 gm Protein • 40 gm Carbohydrate • 328 mg Sodium • 167 mg Calcium • 2 gm Fiber

HE: 1 Bread • 1 Fruit • ½ Fat Free Milk • ½ Fat • ¼ Slider • 15 Optional Calories

Apricot Cobbler

Busy cooks and non-cooks unite: Here's a lovely fruit cobbler that takes no time to prepare but tastes as if you slaved away in the kitchen for ages! It's another one of my pantry pleasers, those recipes that you can make at a moment's notice because the simple ingredients are always on your shelf. *Mmm-mmm!*

● Serves 6

> 1 cup + 2 tablespoons Bisquick Reduced-Fat Baking Mix
> ⅔ cup Carnation Nonfat Dry Milk Powder
> 1 tablespoon Splenda Granular
> ¼ teaspoon ground nutmeg
> ⅓ cup water
> 1 (16-ounce) can apricot halves, packed in fruit juice, undrained

Preheat oven to 400 degrees. In a medium bowl, combine baking mix, dry milk powder, Splenda, nutmeg, and water to form a soft dough. Spread in an ungreased 8-by-8-inch baking dish. Pour undrained apricots over batter. Bake for 25 to 30 minutes. Cut into 6 servings. Serve warm.

HINT: Good with sugar- and fat-free vanilla ice cream, but don't forget to count the additional calories.

Each serving equals:

DIABETIC EXCHANGES: 1 Starch • 1 Fruit

158 Calories • 2 gm Fat • 5 gm Protein •
30 gm Carbohydrate • 306 mg Sodium •
120 mg Calcium • 1 gm Fiber

HE: 1 Bread • ⅔ Fruit • ⅓ Fat Free Milk •
1 Optional Calorie

Cherry Peach Cobbler

Want to win his heart for *sure* this Valentine's Day? Here's my pick for that culinary seduction, a rosy-red, cozy-warm, and utterly delicious dessert that's sweet, spicy, and fragrant—just like you!

○ Serves 6

> 1 (4-serving) package JELL-O sugar-free vanilla cook-and-serve
>   pudding mix
> 1 (4-serving) package JELL-O sugar-free cherry gelatin
> ½ cup water
> 1 (16-ounce) can tart red cherries, packed in water, undrained
> 1 (8-ounce) can sliced peaches, packed in fruit juice, undrained
> 1 (7.5 ounce) can Pillsbury refrigerated buttermilk biscuits
> 2 tablespoons Splenda Granular
> ½ teaspoon ground cinnamon

Preheat oven to 400 degrees. In a medium saucepan, combine dry pudding mix, dry gelatin, and water. Stir in undrained cherries and undrained peaches. Mix gently to combine. Cook over medium heat until mixture thickens and starts to boil, stirring constantly, being careful not to crush the cherries. Remove from heat. Pour hot mixture into an 8-by-8-inch baking dish. Separate biscuits and cut each into 4 pieces. Evenly sprinkle biscuit pieces over hot fruit mixture. Lightly spray top of biscuits with butter-flavored cooking spray. In a small bowl, combine Splenda and cinnamon. Sprinkle mixture evenly over top. Bake for 15 to 18 minutes. Place baking dish on a wire rack and allow to cool. Cut into 6 servings. Good warm or cold.

Each serving equals:

DIABETIC EXCHANGES: 1 Starch • 1 Fruit

157 Calories • 1 gm Fat • 4 gm Protein •
33 gm Carbohydrate • 424 mg Sodium •
14 mg Calcium • 3 gm Fiber

HE: 1¼ Bread • 1 Fruit • ¼ Slider • 2 Optional Calories

Apple Cobbler

Apples cook up so beautifully, they're often at the heart of my coziest recipes, and this classic cobbler is a great example. You'll see that I don't like to peel the skin from my apples, and the reason is simple but important: That skin provides healthy fiber and nutrients we can all use. My daughter-in-law Pam gave this dish an A-plus! ◐ Serves 8

1 (4-serving) package JELL-O sugar-free vanilla cook-and-serve
    pudding mix
1 cup unsweetened apple juice
1 teaspoon apple pie spice ☆
2 cups (6 small) cored, unpeeled, and diced cooking apples
1½ cups Bisquick Reduced-Fat Baking Mix
¼ cup Splenda Granular
¼ cup raisins
½ cup fat-free milk

Preheat oven to 350 degrees. Spray an 8-by-8-inch baking dish with butter-flavored cooking spray. In a medium saucepan, combine dry pudding mix, apple juice, and ½ teaspoon apple pie spice. Stir in apples. Cook over medium heat until mixture thickens and starts to boil, stirring constantly. Pour hot mixture into prepared baking dish. In a medium bowl, combine baking mix, remaining ½ teaspoon apple pie spice, Splenda, and raisins. Add milk. Mix well to combine. Drop by spoonfuls over top of apple mixture. Bake for 30 minutes. Place baking dish on a wire rack and allow to cool. Cut into 8 servings. Good warm or cold.

Each serving equals:

DIABETIC EXCHANGES: 1 Fruit • 1 Starch

137 Calories • 1 gm Fat • 2 gm Protein •
30 gm Carbohydrate • 326 mg Sodium •
37 mg Calcium • 1 gm Fiber

HE: 1 Fruit • 1 Bread • 19 Optional Calories

Tutti-Frutti Coffeecake

Ever since I was a child, I loved saying "Tutti Frutti" aloud. The idea of a dish combining lots of yummy flavors was always so pleasing. Now I've taken that happy memory and woven it into a coffeecake jam-packed with goodies! If you've got the ingredients, it takes very little effort to fix, so maybe you should plan to serve it on a birthday morning as a wake-up surprise!   ☻   Serves 8

1½ cups Bisquick Reduced-Fat Baking Mix
1 (4-serving) package JELL-O sugar-free instant
    vanilla pudding mix
⅔ cup Carnation Nonfat Dry Milk
    Powder
¼ cup chopped walnuts
⅓ cup (1 medium) mashed ripe
    banana
1 egg or equivalent in egg substitute
1 teaspoon vanilla extract
½ cup water
1 (8-ounce) can crushed pineapple, packed in
    fruit juice, undrained
1½ cups fresh blueberries

Preheat oven to 350 degrees. Spray an 8-by-8-inch baking dish with butter-flavored cooking spray. In a large bowl, combine baking mix, dry pudding mix, and dry milk powder. Stir in walnuts. In a small bowl, combine mashed banana, egg, vanilla extract, water, and undrained pineapple. Add banana mixture to baking mix mixture. Mix well to combine. Gently fold in blueberries. Pour mixture into prepared baking dish. Bake for 40 to 45 minutes or until a toothpick inserted in center comes out clean. Place baking dish on a wire rack and allow to cool. Cut into 8 servings.

Each serving equals:

DIABETIC EXCHANGES: 1 Starch/Carbohydrate • 1 Fruit •
½ Fat

184 Calories • 4 gm Fat • 5 gm Protein •
32 gm Carbohydrate • 467 mg Sodium •
100 mg Calcium • 1 gm Fiber

HE: 1 Bread • ¾ Fruit • ¼ Fat Free Milk •
¼ Protein • ¼ Fat • 13 Optional Calories

Apricot Coffeecake

Many people tell me they've never eaten apricots except for the dried kind, so I want to encourage you to seek out the delicious canned varieties now more widely available than ever. They have a luscious flavor all their own, and when you glaze this delectable treat with even more apricot flavor, you'll discover why the juice of the apricot is called *nectar!* ☻ Serves 8

1½ cups Bisquick Reduced-Fat
   Baking Mix
¼ cup Splenda Granular
½ teaspoon ground nutmeg
2 eggs or equivalent in egg
   substitute
1 tablespoon + 1 teaspoon I
   Can't Believe It's Not Butter!
   Light margarine, melted

1 (8-ounce) can crushed
   pineapple, packed in fruit
   juice, drained, and 3
   tablespoons liquid reserved
1 (16-ounce) can apricots,
   packed in fruit juice,
   drained and chopped
6 tablespoons apricot
   spreadable fruit

Preheat oven to 375 degrees. Spray a 9-by-9-inch cake pan with butter-flavored cooking spray. In a large bowl, combine baking mix, Splenda, and nutmeg. Add eggs, melted margarine, and reserved pineapple liquid. Mix well to combine. Blend in apricots and pineapple. Spread batter evenly into prepared cake pan. Bake for 20 to 25 minutes or until golden brown. Place cake pan on a wire rack and allow to cool for 2 to 3 minutes. While still warm, spread spreadable fruit evenly over top. Good served warm or cold.

HINT: Spreadable fruit spreads best at room temperature.

Each serving equals:

DIABETIC EXCHANGES: 1½ Fruit • 1 Starch • ½ Fat

187 Calories • 3 gm Fat • 4 gm Protein •
36 gm Carbohydrate • 289 mg Sodium •
36 mg Calcium • 1 gm Fiber

HE: 1½ Fruit • 1 Bread • ¼ Protein • ¼ Fat •
3 Optional Calories

Hawaiian Upside-Down Coffeecake

There's something fun about baking a dessert that looks absolutely plain when it emerges from the oven, but flip it over and— SURPRISE! You've got a magnificent cake that makes any occasion a celebration. ☉ Serves 8

¾ cup Splenda Granular ☆
2 (8-ounce) cans sliced pineapple, packed in fruit juice, drained, and ½ cup liquid reserved
4 maraschino cherries, halved
1 tablespoon + 1 teaspoon I Can't Believe It's Not Butter! Light margarine
1 egg or equivalent in egg substitute
1 teaspoon vanilla extract
1½ cups Bisquick Reduced-Fat Baking Mix

Preheat oven to 375 degrees. Spray a 9-by-9-inch cake pan with butter-flavored cooking spray. Sprinkle ¼ cup Splenda over bottom. Evenly place pineapple slices on bottom of pan. Place cherry halves in pineapple holes, cut-side up. In a medium bowl, combine margarine and remaining ½ cup Splenda. Add pineapple liquid, egg, and vanilla extract. Mix well to combine using an electric mixer. Add baking mix. Continue beating with mixer for 3 minutes on medium speed. Pour batter over pineapple. Bake for 25 to 30 minutes or until a toothpick inserted in center comes out clean. Loosen sides with a knife and invert immediately onto serving plate. Cut into 8 servings.

Each serving equals:

DIABETIC EXCHANGES: 1 Starch • ½ Fruit • ½ Fat

143 Calories • 3 gm Fat • 2 gm Protein •
27 gm Carbohydrate • 279 mg Sodium •
30 mg Calcium • 1 gm Fiber

HE: 1 Bread • ½ Fruit • ¼ Fat • ¼ Slider •
5 Optional Calories

Raspberry Coffeecake

The cream cheese stirred into the batter for this cake gives the dough a truly scrumptious flavor! This is really more like a raspberry Danish, but so much better tasting than those sticky iced pastries you can buy in any convenience store. It takes a bit more work to roll out the pastry, but the result is definitely worth it!

○ Serves 8

1½ cups Bisquick Reduced-Fat Baking Mix
2 tablespoons Splenda Granular
¾ cup (6 ounces) Philadelphia fat-free
    cream cheese
2 tablespoons Land O Lakes no-fat
    sour cream
1 egg or equivalent in egg substitute
¼ cup fat-free milk
1 tablespoon all-purpose flour
½ cup raspberry spreadable fruit

Preheat oven to 350 degrees. Spray a baking sheet with butter-flavored cooking spray. In a large bowl, combine baking mix, Splenda, cream cheese, and sour cream. Mix well until mixture is crumbly. In a small bowl, combine egg and milk. Add to baking mix mixture. Stir just until moistened. Sprinkle a pastry board or kitchen counter with flour. Place dough on flour and knead 15 to 20 times. Place dough between two slices of waxed paper. Roll into a 12-by-8-inch rectangle. Spread top of dough with spreadable fruit, leaving a ½-inch margin around the edges. Fold each long side to center of dough. Pinch edges to seal. Gently transfer to prepared baking sheet. Make 1-inch cuts about 1 inch apart on each side of coffee cake, cutting ⅓ of the way through the dough at each cut. Bake for 25 to 30 minutes. Place baking sheet on a wire rack and allow to cool. Cut into 8 servings.

HINT: Spreadable fruit spreads best at room temperature.

Each serving equals:

DIABETIC EXCHANGES: 1 Starch/Carbohydrate •
1 Fruit • ½ Meat

---

158 Calories • 2 gm Fat • 6 gm Protein •
29 gm Carbohydrate • 406 mg Sodium •
35 mg Calcium • 0 gm Fiber

HE: 1 Bread • 1 Fruit • ½ Protein •
8 Optional Calories

Peanut Butter and Jelly Coffeecake

Homemade coffeecake sounds like such a splurge, doesn't it? And it's probably something you've rarely, if ever, had time for. That's going to change right now, with a collection of easy-to-fix recipes your friends and family will love! In this one, I took the favorite sandwich of children everywhere and stirred in some of that sweet magic!　　● 　Serves 8

> ⅔ cup Carnation Nonfat Dry Milk Powder
> 1 cup water
> 2 teaspoons white vinegar
> 1½ cups Bisquick Reduced-Fat Baking Mix
> 1 (4-serving) package JELL-O sugar-free instant
>   vanilla pudding mix
> 1 teaspoon baking powder
> ½ teaspoon baking soda
> 6 tablespoons Peter Pan reduced-fat
>   peanut butter
> 1 egg or equivalent in egg substitute
> ¼ cup chopped dry-roasted peanuts ☆
> ½ cup grape spreadable fruit

Preheat oven to 350 degrees. Spray a 9-by-9-inch cake pan with butter-flavored cooking spray. In a small bowl, combine dry milk powder, water, and vinegar. Set aside. In a large bowl, combine baking mix, dry pudding mix, baking powder, and baking soda. Add peanut butter. Mix well using an electric mixer until combined. Add milk mixture and egg. Continue mixing until well blended. Stir in 3 tablespoons peanuts. Spread half of batter into prepared cake pan. Evenly spread spreadable fruit over top. Cover with remaining batter. Evenly sprinkle remaining 1 tablespoon peanuts over top. Bake for 45 to 55 minutes or until a toothpick inserted in center comes out clean. Place cake pan on a wire rack and cool for 5 minutes. Cut into 8 servings.

Each serving equals:

DIABETIC EXCHANGES: 1½ Starch/Carbohydrate •
1 Fruit • ½ Meat

256 Calories • 8 gm Fat • 8 gm Protein •
38 gm Carbohydrate • 740 mg Sodium •
127 mg Calcium • 1 gm Fiber

HE: 1 Bread • 1 Protein • 1 Fat • 1 Fruit •
¼ Fat Free Milk • 13 Optional Calories

Cookies and Brownies Galore

I remember the first Christmas the kids and I moved off the farm. I was so proud that I'd managed to purchase my house all by myself, but money was tight that year. The kids and I baked cookies and packed them in tins as gifts for the very special people who helped us start life over in a house of our own. We made those cookies as a family and delivered them with love. It was all we could afford, but the people who received them knew how much our gift meant.

What I'm trying to say here is that no one should have to live life without cookies!

But too many healthy cookbooks don't understand the role that cookies play in our emotional lives. I mean, doesn't it make you mad when you see a low-fat cookie recipe that tells you that a serving equals one cookie? Anyone who can eat only one cookie probably doesn't need "diet" cookies in the first place!

(I think of my cookie recipes as stopgaps, really, because it's near to impossible to make a great cookie without excessive amounts of fat and sugar. These are the cookies and brownies to eat all year in moderation. Then once or twice a year, enjoy a couple of real sugar cookies.)

I had a letter not long ago from a young mother who said she loved my chocolate chip cookies. She told me she took time out at least twice a week while her kids were napping, and she'd "regroup" by sitting down with three of my chocolate chip cookies and a glass of skim milk, and read for an hour. Maybe it was only an hour, and maybe only twice a week, but I was glad to know my healthier chocolate chip cookies helped her to relax and reenergize. Then, when the kids woke up, it was back to chaos as usual!

Whether you're baking for holiday parties or filling the cookie jar before your grandchildren arrive, these recipes will supply lots of sweet and delicious treats. Isn't it nice that you can bake up a batch of *Pecan Pie Bars* or *Chocolate Peanut Butter Brownies* to bring to a committee meeting—and still partake in the pleasure yourself?

No-Bake Rocky Road Cookies

Here's another recipe you can prepare quickly from your stove-top—and this one blends nuts and marshmallows with yummy chocolate for a soul-satisfying cookie. Trust me: If you're having a rocky day, dig into a couple of these, and it'll be smooth sailing from then on!   ☺   Serves 8 (6 each)

> 2 cups quick oats
> 1/4 cup chopped pecans
> 1 (4-serving) package JELL-O sugar-free chocolate cook-and-serve
>   pudding mix
> 2/3 cup Carnation Nonfat Dry Milk Powder
> 1 cup water
> 1 teaspoon vanilla extract
> 1/2 cup mini marshmallows

In a large bowl, combine oats and pecans. Set aside. In a medium saucepan, combine dry pudding mix, dry milk powder, and water. Cook over medium heat until mixture thickens and starts to boil, stirring constantly. Remove from heat. Add vanilla extract and marshmallows, stirring constantly until marshmallows melt. Pour mixture over oat mixture. Mix well with a fork until well blended. Drop by teaspoonfuls onto waxed paper to form 48 cookies. Let set until firm. Refrigerate leftovers.

Each serving equals:

DIABETIC EXCHANGES: 1 1/2 Starch/Carbohydrate • 1/2 Fat

143 Calories • 3 gm Fat • 6 gm Protein •
23 gm Carbohydrate • 88 mg Sodium •
81 mg Calcium • 2 gm Fiber

HE: 1 Bread • 1/2 Fat • 1/4 Fat Free Milk •
19 Optional Calories

Chocolate Drop Cookies

Too hot to turn on the oven, but your sweet tooth needs a fix? This no-bake recipe uses the top of the stove for just a few minutes, then lets you spoon up a tray of delectable confections in no time at all. Turn up the air conditioner a notch, pour a glass of iced tea, and enjoy! ☺ Serves 8 (6 each)

> 1 (4-serving) package JELL-O sugar-free chocolate cook-and-serve pudding mix
> ⅔ cup Carnation Nonfat Dry Milk Powder
> 1 cup water
> 1 teaspoon vanilla extract
> ½ cup Peter Pan reduced-fat peanut butter
> 2 cups quick oats

In a medium saucepan, combine dry pudding mix, dry milk powder, and water. Cook over medium heat until mixture thickens and starts to boil, stirring constantly. Remove from heat. Stir in vanilla extract, peanut butter, and oats. Drop quickly by teaspoonfuls onto waxed paper to form 48 cookies. Cool until firm.

Each serving equals:

DIABETIC EXCHANGES: 1½ Starch/Carbohydrate • 1 Fat • ½ Meat

---

202 Calories • 6 gm Fat • 10 gm Protein • 27 gm Carbohydrate • 162 mg Sodium • 80 mg Calcium • 3 gm Fiber

---

HE: 1 Fat • 1 Bread • 1 Protein • ¼ Fat Free Milk • 13 Optional Calories

Easy Peanut Butter Cookies

If you're passionate about peanut butter, this cookie has your name on it! Made the traditional way, this homestyle cookie has tons of fat and sugar, but I think you'll agree my "revised" version delivers plenty of peanut butter sizzle in every bite! And you get four, four, four of them in a serving.   ☻   Serves 12 (4 each)

> ½ cup cold water
> 1⅓ cups Carnation Nonfat Dry Milk Powder
> ¾ cup Splenda Granular ☆
> ¾ cup Peter Pan reduced-calorie peanut butter
> 1 egg or equivalent in egg substitute
> 1 teaspoon vanilla extract
> 2 cups Bisquick Reduced-Fat Baking Mix

Place cold water in a 2-cup glass measuring cup. Stir in dry milk powder until mixture makes a smooth paste. Cover and microwave on HIGH (100% power) for 45 to 60 seconds or until mixture is very hot, but not to the boiling point. Stir in ½ cup Splenda. Mix well to combine. Cover and refrigerate at least 2 hours before using. Preheat oven to 350 degrees. Spray a baking sheet with butter-flavored cooking spray. In a large bowl, combine milk mixture, peanut butter, egg, and vanilla extract. Add baking mix. Mix well to combine. Form into 48 (1-inch) balls. Roll balls in remaining ¼ cup Splenda, flatten with bottom of a glass, and make crisscrosses in the center with tines of fork. Bake for 8 to 10 minutes. DO NOT let brown or OVERBAKE. Place baking sheet on a wire rack and allow to cool completely.

Each serving equals:

DIABETIC EXCHANGES: 1½ Starch/Carbohydrate •
1 Fat • ½ Meat

---

195 Calories • 7 gm Fat • 8 gm Protein •
25 gm Carbohydrate • 354 mg Sodium •
111 mg Calcium • 1 gm Fiber

HE: ¾ Bread • ¾ Protein • ⅔ Fat • ⅓ Fat Free Milk •
17 Optional Calories

Chocolate Chip Drops

On a day when you've got something to celebrate, or on one that seems too dreary to survive, the answer is chocolate chip cookies! There's just something about these that says "You're terrific," or "You'll get through this, I promise!" ☻ Serves 12 (4 each)

½ cup cold water
1⅓ cups Carnation Nonfat Dry Milk Powder
½ cup Splenda Granular
1 teaspoon vanilla extract
2¼ cups purchased graham cracker crumbs or
     36 (2½-inch) graham crackers made into crumbs
½ cup mini chocolate chips

Place cold water in a 2-cup glass measuring cup. Stir in dry milk powder until mixture makes a smooth paste. Cover and microwave on HIGH (100% power) for 45 to 60 seconds or until mixture is very hot, but not to the boiling point. Stir in Splenda. Mix well to combine. Cover and refrigerate for at least 2 hours before using. Preheat oven to 350 degrees. Spray baking sheets with butter-flavored cooking spray. In a large bowl, combine milk mixture and vanilla extract. Add graham cracker crumbs and chocolate chips. Drop by teaspoonfuls onto prepared baking sheets to form 48 cookies. Bake for 6 to 7 minutes.

Each serving equals:

DIABETIC EXCHANGES: 2 Starch/Carbohydrate

---

152 Calories • 4 gm Fat • 4 gm Protein •
25 gm Carbohydrate • 178 mg Sodium •
100 mg Calcium • 1 gm Fiber

HE: 1 Bread • ⅓ Fat Free Milk • ¼ Slider •
9 Optional Calories

Peanut Butter Raisin Balls

These are a great summer treat—fruity, nutty, cool, and crunchy. If you're heading for the beach or park, toss some of these into your tote bag. They taste like candy, but they're full of healthy nourishment, so you can enjoy them with a smile.

◐ Serves 4 (4 each)

> ¼ cup Peter Pan reduced-fat peanut butter
> ¼ cup fat-free milk
> ¼ cup raisins
> ¾ cup purchased graham cracker crumbs or
>   12 (2½-inch) graham crackers made into crumbs
> 1 teaspoon vanilla extract
> ¼ teaspoon ground cinnamon

Preheat oven to 350 degrees. Spray a baking sheet with butter-flavored cooking spray. In a medium bowl, cream together peanut butter and milk. Add raisins, graham cracker crumbs, vanilla extract, and cinnamon. Mix well until blended. Form dough into 16 (1-inch) balls. Place balls on prepared baking sheet and slightly flatten. Bake for 5 to 8 minutes. Place baking sheet on a wire rack and allow to cool.

Each serving equals:

DIABETIC EXCHANGES: 1½ Starch/Carbohydrate •
1 Fat • ½ Meat • ½ Fruit

215 Calories • 7 gm Fat • 6 gm Protein •
32 gm Carbohydrate • 220 mg Sodium •
30 mg Calcium • 2 gm Fiber

HE: 1 Bread • 1 Protein • 1 Fat • ½ Fruit

Praline Squares

These are beautifully simple to make, take almost no time to prepare, and will win you cheers from the assembled munchers, whether you stir them up for a class picnic or just a special after-school snack.　　○　Serves 12 (2 each)

24 (2½-inch) graham cracker squares
1 (4-serving) package JELL-O sugar-free vanilla cook-and-serve
　　pudding mix
1¼ cups water
¼ cup Splenda Granular
½ cup chopped pecans

Preheat oven to 425 degrees. Spray a 10-by-15-inch rimmed baking sheet with butter-flavored cooking spray. Arrange graham cracker squares in prepared baking sheet. In a medium saucepan, combine dry pudding mix, water, and Splenda. Cook over medium heat until mixture thickens and starts to boil, stirring constantly. Remove from heat. Stir in pecans. Spread mixture evenly over graham crackers. Bake for 10 minutes. Place baking sheet on a wire rack and allow to cool for 2 to 3 minutes. Cut into 24 squares.

Each serving equals:

DIABETIC EXCHANGES: ½ Starch • ½ Fat

72 Calories • 4 gm Fat • 1 gm Protein •
8 gm Carbohydrate • 83 mg Sodium •
2 mg Calcium • 0 gm Fiber

HE: ⅔ Bread • ½ Fat • 10 Optional Calories

Graham Cracker Crumb Bars

Here's a recipe that's just perfect for you non-cook cooks out there! Mix everything up, pour it in the pan, let it bake, and serve it. What could be easier, tastier, and so much fun? You may even start thinking of yourself as a bit of a baker! ☺ Serves 8 (3 each)

> 2 eggs or equivalent in egg substitute
> ¼ cup Splenda Granular
> 3 tablespoons fat-free milk
> 1 teaspoon vanilla extract
> ¼ cup chopped pecans
> 1½ cups purchased graham cracker crumbs or
>   24 (2½-inch) graham crackers made into crumbs

Preheat oven to 350 degrees. Spray a 9-by-13-inch baking dish with butter-flavored cooking spray. In a large bowl, combine eggs, Splenda, milk, and vanilla extract. Mix well using an electric mixer. Blend in pecans and graham cracker crumbs. Spread into prepared baking dish. Bake for 12 to 14 minutes. Cut into 24 bars while still warm.

Each serving equals:

DIABETIC EXCHANGES: 1½ Starch • 1 Fat

166 Calories • 6 gm Fat • 4 gm Protein •
24 gm Carbohydrate • 200 mg Sodium •
22 mg Calcium • 1 gm Fiber

HE: 1 Bread • ½ Fat • ¼ Protein • 5 Optional Calories

Pineapple Carrot Bars

I thought, why not make a great carrot cake as a bar cookie, and so I created this fast and fabulous recipe. I think they're even better after they've "rested" overnight, so I'd recommend making them the day before you plan to serve them. My grandson Zach smiled so happily when nibbling one of these, I felt all warm inside.

● Serves 8 (3 each)

1 cup + 2 tablespoons all-
   purpose flour
1 teaspoon baking powder
1 teaspoon baking soda
1 teaspoon ground
   cinnamon
⅓ cup Splenda Granular
1 cup finely grated
   carrots

1 (8-ounce) can crushed
   pineapple, packed in fruit
   juice, drained, and liquid
   reserved
¼ cup chopped walnuts
1 egg or equivalent in egg
   substitute
1 teaspoon vanilla extract
2 tablespoons vegetable oil

Preheat oven to 350 degrees. Spray a 9-by-13-inch cake pan with butter-flavored cooking spray. In a medium bowl, combine flour, baking powder, baking soda, cinnamon, and Splenda. Stir in carrots, pineapple, and walnuts. Add enough water to reserved pineapple liquid to make ⅓ cup liquid. Pour liquid into a small bowl. Add egg, vanilla extract, and oil. Mix well to combine. Add liquid mixture to flour mixture. Mix gently to combine. Spread batter evenly into prepared cake pan. Bake for 25 minutes. Place cake pan on a wire rack and allow to cool. Cut into 24 bars.

Each serving equals:

DIABETIC EXCHANGES: 1½ Starch/Carbohydrate • 1 Fat

150 Calories • 6 gm Fat • 3 gm Protein •
21 gm Carbohydrate • 232 mg Sodium •
55 mg Calcium • 1 gm Fiber

HE: 1 Fat • ¾ Bread • ¼ Fruit • ¼ Vegetable •
¼ Protein • 5 Optional Calories

Lemon Coconut Bars

If you've always participated in a cookie exchange, but aren't sure you still can now that you're cooking the Healthy Exchanges way, why not share this section with your friends, and make your New Year's resolutions early this year? Everyone can choose one recipe (this one's a true delight!) and then you all get a chance to try each one!   ☺   Serves 12 (2 each)

> 1 (8-ounce) can Pillsbury Reduced-Fat
>   Crescent Rolls
> 1 (8-ounce) package Philadelphia fat-free
>   cream cheese
> 2 tablespoons Splenda Granular
> ½ teaspoon coconut extract
> 2 (8-ounce) cans crushed pineapple, packed in fruit juice,
>   drained, and ⅓ cup liquid reserved
> 1 cup water
> 1 (4-serving) package JELL-O sugar-free lemon gelatin
> 1 (4-serving) package JELL-O sugar-free vanilla
>   cook-and-serve pudding mix
> 3 tablespoons flaked coconut

Preheat oven to 405 degrees. Spray a 9-by-13-inch rimmed baking pan with butter-flavored cooking spray. Pat rolls into prepared baking pan being sure to seal perforations. Bake for 5 to 7 minutes or until light golden brown. Place baking pan on a wire rack and allow to cool. In a medium bowl, stir cream cheese with a spoon until soft. Add Splenda, coconut extract, and pineapple. Spread mixture evenly over cooled crust. In a medium saucepan, combine reserved pineapple liquid, water, dry gelatin, and dry pudding mix. Cook over medium heat until mixture thickens and starts to boil, stirring constantly. Evenly spoon hot liquid over cream cheese mixture. Refrigerate for at least 1 hour. Sprinkle coconut evenly over top. Cut into 24 servings. Refrigerate leftovers.

Each serving equals:

DIABETIC EXCHANGES: 1 Starch/Carbohydrate • ½ Fat

119 Calories • 3 gm Fat • 5 gm Protein •
18 gm Carbohydrate • 326 mg Sodium •
6 gm Calcium • 0 gm Fiber

HE: ⅔ Bread • ⅓ Protein • ⅓ Fruit •
15 Optional Calories

Magical Fruit Cake Bars

Fruitcake gets such a bad rap, and comedians tell awful jokes about it, but the truth is, if you make it right, it's great! These are genuinely rich, with the hearty blend of fruits, nuts, and two flavorful extracts. When we asked our taste testers what they thought, we got jokes before they tried 'em—and *mmm-mmms* after!

● Serves 8 (2 each)

> ½ cup cold water
> 1⅓ cups Carnation Nonfat Dry Milk Powder
> ½ cup Splenda Granular
> 1 teaspoon lemon juice
> 1 teaspoon coconut extract
> 1 teaspoon rum extract
> 1½ cups purchased graham cracker crumbs or 24 (2½-inch)
>   graham crackers made into crumbs
> 1 (16-ounce) can fruit cocktail, packed in fruit juice, drained
> ½ cup raisins
> 2 tablespoons flaked coconut
> 2 tablespoons chopped pecans

Place cold water in a 2-cup glass measuring cup. Stir in dry milk powder until mixture makes a smooth paste. Cover and microwave on HIGH (100% power) for 45 to 60 seconds or until mixture is very hot, but not to the boiling point. Stir in Splenda. Mix well to combine. Cover and refrigerate for at least 2 hours before using. Preheat oven to 350 degrees. Spray an 8-by-8-inch baking dish with butter-flavored cooking spray. In a large bowl, combine lemon juice, coconut extract, rum extract, and milk mixture. Stir in graham cracker crumbs. Add fruit cocktail and raisins. Mix well to combine. Spread mixture into prepared baking dish. Evenly sprinkle coconut and pecans over top. Bake for 30 to 35 minutes or until lightly browned. Place baking dish on a wire rack and allow to cool. Cut into 16 bars. Store leftovers loosely in a covered container.

Each serving equals:

DIABETIC EXCHANGES: 1 Starch/Carbohydrate •
1 Fruit • ½ Fat Free Milk • ½ Fat

212 Calories • 4 gm Fat • 6 gm Protein •
38 gm Carbohydrate • 205 mg Sodium •
155 mg Calcium • 2 gm Fiber

HE: 1 Bread • 1 Fruit • ½ Fat Free Milk • ¼ Fat •
10 Optional Calories

Pecan Pie Bars

It's the taste of the South—chewy, scrumptious, downright decadent—and now it can be yours without the extra fat and sugar! If you bring these bars to a holiday bash, you'll be the most popular cook on the block. ☺ Serves 8 (2 each)

1 (8-ounce) can Pillsbury Reduced-Fat Crescent Rolls
1 (4-serving) package JELL-O sugar-free vanilla cook-and-serve
pudding mix
⅔ cup Carnation Nonfat Dry Milk Powder
1½ cups water
2 teaspoons vanilla extract
½ cup chopped pecans

Preheat oven to 350 degrees. Pat rolls into an ungreased 10-by-15-inch rimmed baking sheet. Gently press dough to cover bottom of pan, being sure to seal perforations. Bake for 5 minutes. In a medium saucepan, combine dry pudding mix, dry milk powder, and water. Cook over medium heat until mixture thickens and starts to boil, stirring constantly. Add vanilla extract and pecans. Spread mixture evenly over partially baked crust and continue baking for 15 to 20 minutes. Place baking sheet on a wire rack and allow to cool. Cut into 16 bars.

Each serving equals:

DIABETIC EXCHANGES: 1½ Starch/Carbohydrate • 1 Fat

177 Calories • 9 gm Fat • 5 gm Protein •
19 gm Carbohydrate • 321 mg Sodium •
72 mg Calcium • 0 gm Fiber

HE: 1 Bread • 1 Fat • ¼ Fat Free Milk •
10 Optional Calories

Pumpkin Chocolate Chip Bars

Are you starting to think that I might own a piece of a pumpkin farm? There are quite a few pumpkin recipes in this book, I admit it, but few ingredients add more flavor, texture, and moisture to a recipe than that old "jack-o'-lantern stuffing." Of course, I prefer mine from a can!   ☻   Serves 12 (3 each)

1½ cups all-purpose flour
1 teaspoon baking powder
½ teaspoon baking soda
2 teaspoons pumpkin pie spice
¾ cup Splenda Granular
1 (15-ounce) can solid-packed
   pumpkin

3 eggs, beaten, or equivalent in
   egg substitute
3 tablespoons vegetable oil
1 teaspoon vanilla extract
¼ cup water
¼ cup mini chocolate chips

Preheat oven to 350 degrees. Spray a 10-by-15-inch rimmed baking sheet with butter-flavored cooking spray. In a large bowl, combine flour, baking powder, baking soda, pumpkin pie spice, and Splenda. In a medium bowl, combine pumpkin, eggs, oil, vanilla extract, and water. Add pumpkin mixture to flour mixture. Mix just until moistened. Stir in chocolate chips. Evenly spread mixture into prepared baking sheet. Bake for 30 minutes or until a toothpick inserted in center comes out clean. Place baking sheet on a wire rack and allow to cool. Cut into 36 bars.

Each serving equals:

DIABETIC EXCHANGES: 1 Fat • 1 Starch/Carbohydrate

129 Calories • 5 gm Fat • 4 gm Protein •
17 gm Carbohydrate • 112 mg Sodium •
45 mg Calcium • 2 gm Fiber

HE: ¾ Fat • ⅔ Bread • ⅓ Vegetable • ¼ Protein •
¼ Slider

Chocolate Peanut Butter Brownies

This wonderfully nutty recipe celebrates the great relationship that peanut butter and chocolate have always enjoyed (evidence: the peanut butter cup!). This tasty mix produces a more cakelike brownie because of the eggs. ☻ Serves 8 (2 each)

¾ cup all-purpose flour
¼ cup unsweetened cocoa
1 teaspoon baking powder
½ teaspoon baking soda
½ cup Splenda Granular
2 eggs or equivalent in egg substitute

6 tablespoons Peter Pan reduced-fat peanut butter
1 teaspoon vanilla extract
2 teaspoons vegetable oil
⅔ cup Land O Lakes no-fat sour cream
¼ cup mini chocolate chips

Preheat oven to 350 degrees. Spray an 8-by-8-inch baking dish with butter-flavored cooking spray. In a medium bowl, combine flour, cocoa, baking powder, baking soda, and Splenda. In a small bowl, combine eggs, peanut butter, vanilla extract, oil, and sour cream. Mix well with a wire whisk until blended. Add egg mixture to flour mixture. Stir well until just combined. Evenly spread mixture into prepared baking dish. Bake for 25 to 30 minutes. Sprinkle chocolate chips evenly over top. Continue baking for 2 to 3 minutes. Place baking dish on a wire rack and allow to cool. Cut into 16 bars.

Each serving equals:

DIABETIC EXCHANGES: 1 Meat • 1 Fat • 1 Starch/Carbohydrate

184 Calories • 8 gm Fat • 7 gm Protein • 21 gm Carbohydrate • 239 mg Sodium • 67 mg Calcium • 2 gm Fiber

HE: 1 Protein • 1 Fat • ½ Bread • ½ Slider • 5 Optional Calories

Double Chocolate Walnut Brownies

Don't you just love the idea of adding chocolate chips to a brownie batter? Think how they'll melt during baking and ooze that chocolatey goodness all through—wait, don't get carried away just yet! Let the brownies cool before you're tempted to devour them.

○ Serves 8 (2 each)

1½ cups all-purpose flour
¾ cup Splenda Granular
¼ cup unsweetened cocoa
1 teaspoon baking powder
½ teaspoon baking soda
½ cup chopped walnuts

¼ cup mini chocolate chips
½ cup plain fat-free yogurt
⅓ cup Kraft fat-free
    mayonnaise
1 teaspoon vanilla extract
¾ cup water

Preheat oven to 350 degrees. Spray a 9-by-13-inch cake pan with butter-flavored cooking spray. In a large bowl, combine flour, Splenda, cocoa, baking powder, and baking soda. Stir in walnuts and chocolate chips. In a medium bowl, combine yogurt, mayonnaise, vanilla extract, and water. Mix well with a wire whisk until blended. Add yogurt mixture to flour mixture. Mix gently just to combine. Spread batter evenly into prepared cake pan. Bake for 15 to 20 minutes or until a toothpick inserted in center comes out clean. Place cake pan on a wire rack and allow to cool for at least 15 minutes. Cut into 16 brownies.

Each serving equals:

DIABETIC EXCHANGES: 1½ Starch/Carbohydrate • 1 Fat

182 Calories • 6 gm Fat • 5 gm Protein • 27 gm Carbohydrate • 287 mg Sodium • 61 mg Calcium • 2 gm Fiber

HE: 1 Bread • ½ Fat • ¼ Protein • ½ Slider • 4 Optional Calories

Cherry Fudge Brownies

If you've loved chocolate-covered cherries since childhood, here's a fun recipe to try that brings together those delicious flavors in a rich brownie bar. I know you'll be tempted, but do let them cool for a little while so you won't burn your lips. The taste gets better and better, and they're terrific the next day!

● Serves 8 (2 each)

> 1 (4-serving) package JELL-O sugar-free chocolate cook-and-serve pudding mix
> 1 (4-serving) package JELL-O sugar-free cherry gelatin
> 1½ cups water ☆
> 1 (16-ounce) can tart red cherries, packed in water, drained
> ¾ cup all-purpose flour
> 1 teaspoon baking powder
> ½ teaspoon baking soda
> ½ cup Splenda Granular
> ¼ cup unsweetened cocoa
> ⅔ cup Carnation Nonfat Dry Milk Powder
> 1 teaspoon lemon juice
> 1 teaspoon vanilla extract

Preheat oven to 350 degrees. Spray a 9-by-9-inch cake pan with butter-flavored cooking spray. In a medium saucepan, combine dry pudding mix, dry gelatin, and 1 cup water. Stir in cherries. Cook over medium heat until mixture thickens and starts to boil, stirring often, being careful not to crush the cherries. Remove from heat. Meanwhile, in a large bowl, combine flour, baking powder, baking soda, Splenda, and cocoa. In a small bowl, combine dry milk powder and remaining ½ cup water. Stir in lemon juice and vanilla extract. Add milk mixture to flour mixture. Mix gently to combine. Gently fold in partially cooled cherry mixture. Spread mixture evenly into prepared cake pan. Bake for 25 to 30 minutes or until a toothpick inserted in center comes out clean. Place cake pan on a wire rack and let cool about 15 minutes. Cut into 16 bars.

Each serving equals:

DIABETIC EXCHANGES: 1 Starch/Carbohydrate • ½ Fruit

112 Calories • 0 gm Fat • 5 gm Protein •
23 gm Carbohydrate • 368 mg Sodium •
115 mg Calcium • 2 gm Fiber

HE: ½ Bread • ½ Fruit • ¼ Fat Free Milk •
¼ Slider • 8 Optional Calories

4-13-08   *Not Good.*

Cliff's Double Treat Chocolate Brownies

If people are born with a gene that encourages them to seek out chocolate anywhere and everywhere, I'd be willing to bet that Cliff has double the usual number! He's got plenty of company, of course, in the chocolate lovers' club (are you a member?) and so, this one's for all of you! ☻ Serves 8 (2 each)

¾ cup all-purpose flour
¼ cup unsweetened cocoa
¼ cup mini chocolate chips
½ cup Splenda Granular
¼ cup chopped walnuts
1 egg or equivalent in egg substitute

½ cup Land O Lakes no-fat sour cream
¼ cup water
1 teaspoon vanilla extract

Preheat oven to 325 degrees. Spray an 8-by-8-inch baking dish with butter-flavored cooking spray. In a large bowl, combine flour, cocoa, chocolate chips, and Splenda. Stir in walnuts. Add egg, sour cream, water, and vanilla extract. Mix well to combine. Spread mixture into prepared baking dish. Bake for 22 to 25 minutes or just until the edges are firm and the center is almost set. Place baking dish on a wire rack and allow to cool. Cut into 16 servings.

Each serving equals:

DIABETIC EXCHANGES: 1 Starch/Carbohydrate • ½ Fat

120 Calories • 4 gm Fat • 4 gm Protein •
17 gm Carbohydrate • 30 mg Sodium •
30 gm Calcium • 2 gm Fiber

HE: ½ Bread • ¼ Protein • ¼ Fat • ½ Slider •
7 Optional Calories

More, More, More
of the Good Stuff

My grandma ran a boardinghouse, and until the day she died at the age of ninety (in 1955), she was still cooking on a wood-burning cookstove. The "good stuff" that came out of her oven was just as fabulous as any masterpiece painted by the old masters. Especially her Banana Bread!

She took the old rotten bananas that most people would toss, and she'd end up with a sweet banana bread that was to die for. That warm, walnutty bread was so good, I can still taste it in my mind. My grandmother had a black walnut tree in her backyard, and we always used to gather walnuts in the fall. We'd grind the shells off in the corn husker, and then sit around her woodstove picking out the nuts and putting them in jars so we'd have them all year long.

I know that's why nuts—in tiny amounts where my eyes can eat them and my taste buds can enjoy them—are important to me. I use just enough so that when you bite in you can hear and taste the crunch, and you think you're getting more than you are. My grandma would have put a whole cup of walnuts in her banana bread, while I only use a quarter cup, but it's enough to bring those sweet times back.

I'm giving you more terrific Healthy Exchanges recipes that both look and taste good—not like so many of the low-fat recipes I've tried and discarded. Do *Peanut Butter and Jelly Muffins* sound good? How about *Strawberry Daiquiri Sundaes* and *Cherry Pretzel Torte?* I had so many luscious ideas that didn't fit the other sections, I just had to make room for them.

Here are delectable dessert pancakes taste-tested by my grandsons, Zach and Josh, who love sitting in my kitchen with "Papa" Cliff and enjoying treats that I've made special with just a little extra work. For me, good enough will never be good enough again! You asked for more, more, more—well, here it is!

Double Layer Lemon Dessert

There's just something about a lemon dessert that make you feel light and a little bit virtuous! This one is gorgeously creamy, and the touch of coconut on top is not only pretty but tasty too. Be careful with your boxes of pudding, now—the cook and serve looks a lot like instant, and vice versa! ☻ Serves 8

12 (2½-inch) graham cracker
    squares ☆
2 (4-serving) packages JELL-O
    sugar-free lemon gelatin ☆
1 (4-serving) package JELL-O
    sugar-free vanilla cook-
    and-serve pudding mix
2½ cups water ☆

1 (4-serving) package JELL-O
    sugar-free instant vanilla
    pudding mix
⅔ cup Carnation Nonfat Dry
    Milk Powder
¾ cup Cool Whip Free
1 teaspoon coconut extract
2 tablespoons flaked coconut

Evenly arrange 10 graham cracker squares in an 11-by-7-inch biscuit pan. In a medium saucepan, combine 1 package dry gelatin, dry cook-and-serve pudding mix, and 1½ cups water. Cook over medium heat until mixture thickens and starts to boil, stirring often. Remove from heat and allow to cool 2 to 3 minutes. Pour pudding mixture evenly over graham crackers. Refrigerate for at least 30 minutes. In a medium bowl, combine remaining dry gelatin, dry instant pudding mix, dry milk powder, and remaining 1 cup water. Mix well using a wire whisk. Blend in Cool Whip Free and coconut extract. Spread mixture evenly over set lemon layer. Finely crush remaining 2 graham crackers. In a small bowl, combine cracker crumbs and coconut. Evenly sprinkle mixture over top. Refrigerate for at least 15 minutes. Cut into 8 servings.

Each serving equals:

DIABETIC EXCHANGES: 1 Starch/Carbohydrate

89 Calories • 1 gm Fat • 4 gm Protein •
16 gm Carbohydrate • 348 mg Sodium •
69 mg Calcium • 0 gm Fiber

HE: ½ Bread • ¼ Fat Free Milk • ½ Slider •
7 Optional Calories

Orange Slices in Orange Custard Sauce

Here's an inexpensive, last-minute dessert that looks beautifully festive and tastes as if you fussed! It's important to choose unbruised seedless fruit for this, firm to the touch but not hard.

○ Serves 6

> 4 (medium-sized) navel oranges
> 1 (4-serving) package JELL-O sugar-free vanilla cook-and-serve
>   pudding mix
> 1 cup Carnation Nonfat Dry Milk Powder
> 1 cup unsweetened orange juice
> 1 cup water
> 1 teaspoon vanilla extract
> 1 tablespoon mini chocolate chips

Peel oranges and cut each into 4 thick, round slices. Remove center pith. Set aside. In a medium saucepan, combine dry pudding mix, dry milk powder, orange juice, and water. Cook over medium heat until mixture thickens and starts to boil, stirring constantly. Remove from heat. Stir in vanilla extract. Spread about 2 tablespoons hot sauce on 6 dessert plates. Evenly arrange orange slices over sauce on plates. Spoon about ⅓ cup sauce over each. Sprinkle ½ teaspoon chocolate chips over top of each. Serve at once.

Each serving equals:

DIABETIC EXCHANGES: 1 Fruit • ½ Fat Free Milk

124 Calories • 0 gm Fat • 5 gm Protein •
26 gm Carbohydrate • 139 mg Sodium •
192 mg Calcium • 2 gm Fiber

HE: 1 Fruit • ½ Fat Free Milk • ¼ Slider •
18 Optional Calories

Triple Decker Dessert

High, higher, highest—why settle for anything less? Each layer of this astonishingly yummy combo is scrumptious on its own, but when you have them join hands in one gorgeous creation, you've got a perfect party on a plate! ☻ Serves 8

12 (2½-inch) graham cracker squares ☆
1 (8-ounce) package Philadelphia fat-free cream cheese
1 tablespoon fat-free milk
1 teaspoon vanilla extract
2 tablespoons Splenda Granular
1 (4-serving) package JELL-O sugar-free instant butterscotch
    pudding mix
1⅓ cups Carnation Nonfat Dry Milk Powder ☆
2½ cups water ☆
1 (4-serving) package JELL-O sugar-free instant chocolate
    pudding mix
1 cup Cool Whip Lite
1 teaspoon coconut extract
2 tablespoons flaked coconut
1 tablespoon mini chocolate chips

Place 9 graham cracker squares in a 9-by-9-inch cake pan. In a small bowl, stir cream cheese with a spoon until soft. Stir in milk, vanilla extract, and Splenda. Spread cream cheese mixture evenly over graham crackers. In a medium bowl, combine dry butterscotch pudding mix, ⅔ cup dry milk powder, and 1¼ cups water. Mix well using a wire whisk. Pour butterscotch mixture evenly over cream cheese mixture. In same bowl, combine dry chocolate pudding mix, remaining ⅔ cup dry milk powder, and remaining 1¼ cups water. Mix well using a wire whisk. Pour chocolate mixture over butterscotch mixture. Refrigerate for 5 minutes. In a small bowl, combine Cool Whip Lite and coconut extract. Spread Cool Whip Lite mixture evenly over chocolate layer. Crush remaining 3 graham cracker squares and sprinkle evenly over Cool Whip Lite.

Evenly sprinkle coconut and chocolate chips over top. Refrigerate for at least 2 hours. Cut into 8 servings.

Each serving equals:

DIABETIC EXCHANGES: 1 Starch/Carbohydrate • ½ Meat • ½ Fat Free Milk

---

167 Calories • 3 gm Fat • 9 gm Protein • 26 gm Carbohydrate • 653 mg Sodium • 142 mg Calcium • 0 gm Fiber

---

HE: ½ Bread • ½ Protein • ½ Fat Free Milk • ½ Slider • 17 Optional Calories

Black Forest Dessert

This is one of those recipes I created when I didn't have a piecrust on hand but wanted to make a pie. By using graham crackers to make a tasty crust—necessity—I became the "Mother of Invention"! Too bad I can't patent this particular inspiration (I'd be rich!), but I'm pleased to share it with you!   ☻   Serves 8

12 (2½-inch) chocolate graham cracker squares ☆

1 (4-serving) package JELL-O sugar-free cherry gelatin

1 (4-serving) package JELL-O sugar-free vanilla cook-and-serve
    pudding mix

1 (16-ounce) can tart red cherries, packed in water, drained, and
    ⅓ cup liquid reserved

2 cups water ☆

1½ cups plain fat-free yogurt

⅔ cup Carnation Nonfat Dry Milk Powder

1 teaspoon vanilla extract

2 (4-serving) packages JELL-O sugar-free instant chocolate
    pudding mix

Place 9 chocolate graham crackers in a 9-by-9-inch cake pan. In a medium saucepan, combine dry gelatin and dry vanilla cook-and-serve pudding mix. Add reserved cherry liquid and 1 cup water. Mix well to combine. Stir in cherries. Cook over medium heat until mixture thickens and starts to boil, stirring constantly, being careful not to crush the cherries. Remove from heat. Place saucepan on a wire rack and allow to cool. Meanwhile, combine yogurt, dry milk powder, remaining 1 cup water, and vanilla extract. Add dry instant pudding mixes. Mix well using a wire whisk. Spread mixture evenly over graham crackers. Refrigerate for 15 minutes. Spoon cooled cherry mixture evenly over chocolate pudding mixture. Crush remaining 3 chocolate graham crackers. Evenly sprinkle crumbs over cherries. Refrigerate for at least 1 hour. Cut into 8 servings.

Each serving equals:

DIABETIC EXCHANGES: 1 Starch/Carbohydrate •
½ Fat Free Milk • ½ Fruit

161 Calories • 1 gm Fat • 7 gm Protein •
31 gm Carbohydrate • 565 mg Sodium •
167 mg Calcium • 1 gm Fiber

HE: ½ Bread • ½ Fat Free Milk • ½ Fruit •
½ Slider • 5 Optional Calories

Margarita Pretzel Salad Dessert

Even if you've never tasted a true margarita, you'll still enjoy this refreshing treat that echoes its tangy lime flavor! It's wonderfully rich, delightfully creamy—and you might just shout "Olé!"

◐ Serves 8

> 1 cup crushed pretzels ☆
>
> ½ cup Splenda Granular ☆
>
> 2 tablespoons + 2 teaspoons I Can't Believe It's Not Butter! Light margarine, melted
>
> 1 (8-ounce) package Philadelphia fat-free cream cheese
>
> 1 cup Cool Whip Lite ☆
>
> 1 (4-serving) package JELL-O sugar-free lime gelatin
>
> 1 (4-serving) package JELL-O sugar-free instant vanilla pudding mix
>
> ⅔ cup Carnation Nonfat Dry Milk Powder
>
> 1⅓ cups water

Preheat oven to 400 degrees. Reserve 2 tablespoons crushed pretzels. In a medium bowl, combine remaining pretzels, ¼ cup Splenda, and melted margarine. Pat mixture into an 8-by-8-inch baking dish. Bake for 10 minutes. Place baking dish on a wire rack and allow to cool. In a medium bowl, stir cream cheese with a spoon until soft. Add remaining ¼ cup Splenda and ¼ cup Cool Whip Lite. Evenly spread mixture over cooled pretzel crust. In a medium bowl, combine dry gelatin, dry pudding mix, and dry milk powder. Add water. Mix well using a wire whisk. Spread mixture evenly over cream cheese mixture. Refrigerate for about 30 minutes. Evenly spread remaining ¾ cup Cool Whip Lite over set pudding mixture. Sprinkle remaining 2 tablespoons crushed pretzels evenly over top. Refrigerate for about 30 minutes. Cut into 8 servings.

HINT: A self-seal sandwich bag works great for crushing pretzels.

Each serving equals:

DIABETIC EXCHANGES: 1½ Starch/Carbohydrate • ½ Fat

---

191 Calories • 3 gm Fat • 9 gm Protein •
32 gm Carbohydrate • 898 mg Sodium •
79 mg Calcium • 1 gm Fiber

HE: ½ Fat • ½ Protein • ⅓ Bread • ¼ Fat Free Milk •
¼ Slider • 17 Optional Calories

Chocolate Raspberry Meringues

Elegant but surprisingly easy, this lovely dessert is an excellent choice for your next very special occasion! Because the meringues can be prepared in advance, you won't be stuck in the kitchen while your guests visit with one another. (By the way, you should be able to find parchment paper for this recipe at any kitchen supply store.)

◐ Serves 6

6 egg whites
¾ cup Splenda Granular ☆
1½ teaspoons almond extract ☆
¼ cup chopped almonds
2 tablespoons mini chocolate chips
1 (4-serving) package JELL-O sugar-free instant chocolate
   pudding mix
⅔ cup Carnation Nonfat Dry Milk Powder
1¼ cups water
¾ cup Cool Whip Free ☆
1½ cups frozen unsweetened raspberries, thawed
   and undrained

Preheat oven to 325 degrees. In a large bowl, beat egg whites on HIGH with an electric mixer until soft peaks form. Gradually add ½ cup Splenda and 1 teaspoon almond extract, beating on HIGH until stiff peaks form. Fold in almonds and chocolate chips. Place parchment paper on a jelly roll pan. Form 6 even mounds. Form mounds into 4-inch circles, forming a rim around edges. Bake for 20 to 25 minutes. Remove from oven. Place baking pan on a wire rack and allow to cool completely. Remove from paper. Place on dessert plates. In a medium bowl, combine dry pudding mix, dry milk powder, and water. Mix well using a wire whisk. Blend in ¼ cup Cool Whip Free. Evenly spoon mixture into cooled meringues. Top each with 1 heaping tablespoon Cool Whip Free. In a small bowl, combine thawed raspberries and remaining ¼ cup Splenda. Blend in remaining ½ teaspoon almond extract. Evenly spoon about ¼ cup raspberry mixture over top of each. Refrigerate until ready to serve.

Each serving equals:

DIABETIC EXCHANGES: 1 Starch/Carbohydrate • 1 Fat • ½ Meat

144 Calories • 4 gm Fat • 8 gm Protein • 19 gm Carbohydrate • 322 mg Sodium • 115 mg Calcium • 1 gm Fiber

HE: ½ Protein • ⅓ Fat • ⅓ Fat Free Milk • ⅓ Fruit • ½ Slider • 19 Optional Calories

Chocolate Mint Sin

The name of this recipe is a bit tongue-in-cheek, because this book celebrates sinful-looking but sinless desserts. If you close your eyes and imagine what a dessert called "Sin" might taste like, I hope this is what you dreamed about! It's one sin you can enjoy without guilt, I promise!　　○　Serves 12

1½ cups all-purpose flour
¼ cup unsweetened cocoa
½ cup Splenda Granular
1⅔ cups Carnation
　　Nonfat Dry Milk
　　Powder ☆
1 teaspoon baking powder
½ teaspoon baking soda
⅔ cup Kraft fat-free
　　mayonnaise
1 cup cold coffee
1 teaspoon mint extract

2 (4-serving) packages JELL-O
　　sugar-free instant
　　chocolate pudding mix
3 cups water
¾ cup plain fat-free yogurt
1½ cups Cool Whip Lite ☆
6 tablespoons chopped
　　pecans ☆
12 (2½-inch) chocolate
　　graham cracker squares
　　made into crumbs ☆
3 to 4 drops green food coloring

Preheat oven to 350 degrees. Spray a 9-by-9-inch cake pan with butter-flavored cooking spray. In a large bowl, combine flour, cocoa, Splenda, ⅓ cup dry milk powder, baking powder, and baking soda. Add mayonnaise, coffee, and mint extract. Mix well to combine. Pour batter into prepared cake pan. Bake for 18 to 22 minutes or until a toothpick inserted in center comes out clean. Place cake pan on a wire rack and allow to cool completely. Cut cake into 36 pieces. Layer half of cake pieces in a decorative glass bowl. In a large bowl, combine dry pudding mix, remaining 1⅓ cups dry milk powder, and water. Mix well using a wire whisk. Blend in yogurt and ¾ cup Cool Whip Lite. Spread half of pudding mixture over cake cubes. Sprinkle 3 tablespoons pecans over pudding layer. Reserve 4 tablespoons chocolate graham cracker crumbs. Evenly sprinkle remaining crumbs over pecans. Repeat layers with cake cubes and pudding mixture. In a small bowl, combine remaining ¾ cup Cool Whip Lite and green food coloring. Evenly drop topping mixture over top to form 12 mounds. Evenly sprinkle remaining 3 tablespoons pecans and 4 tablespoons graham cracker crumbs over top. Cover and refrigerate for at least 1 hour. Cut into 12 servings.

Each serving equals:

DIABETIC EXCHANGES: 1½ Starch/Carbohydrate • ½ Fat Free Milk • ½ Fat

188 Calories • 4 gm Fat • 7 gm Protein • 31 gm Carbohydrate • 504 mg Sodium • 155 mg Calcium • 2 gm Fiber

HE: 1 Bread • ½ Fat Free Milk • ½ Fat • ½ Slider • 18 Optional Calories

Raspberry Isle Layered Dessert

It's true that I'm wild about strawberries, but raspberries have their own special pizzazz! This dish piles so much fruity, creamy flavor sky-high, your spirits will rise after just one taste. ☻ Serves 6

12 (2½-inch) chocolate graham
    cracker squares ☆
1 (8-ounce) package
    Philadelphia fat-free
    cream cheese
2 tablespoons Splenda
    Granular
¾ cup Cool Whip Free
1 teaspoon coconut
    extract

1 (4-serving) package JELL-O
    sugar-free vanilla cook-
    and-serve pudding mix
1 (4-serving) package JELL-O
    sugar-free raspberry
    gelatin
1 cup water
1½ cups frozen unsweetened
    raspberries
2 tablespoons flaked coconut

Arrange 9 graham crackers in the bottom of a 9-by-9-inch cake pan. In a large bowl, stir cream cheese with a spoon until soft. Add Splenda, Cool Whip Free, and coconut extract. Mix gently to combine. Evenly spread cream cheese mixture over graham crackers. Refrigerate while preparing raspberry sauce. In a medium saucepan, combine dry pudding mix, dry gelatin, and water. Cook over medium heat until mixture thickens and starts to boil, stirring often. Remove from heat. Gently stir in raspberries. Place saucepan on a wire rack and let set for 15 minutes. Spoon raspberry sauce evenly over cream cheese layer. Crush remaining 3 chocolate graham crackers. Evenly sprinkle graham cracker crumbs and coconut over top. Cover and refrigerate for at least 2 hours. Cut into 6 servings.

Each serving equals:

DIABETIC EXCHANGES: 1 Starch/Carbohydrate •
½ Meat • ½ Fruit

113 Calories • 1 gm Fat • 7 gm Protein •
19 gm Carbohydrate • 393 mg Sodium •
7 mg Calcium • 1 gm Fiber

HE: ⅔ Bread • ⅔ Protein • ⅓ Fruit • ½ Slider •
2 Optional Calories

Strawberry Daiquiri Sundaes

Most sundae toppings are very high in sugar and some are also high in fat, so I wanted to create a dazzling and delicious way to crown your favorite flavor of healthy ice cream. I admit it—in my book, this is definitely a taste of heaven! ☻ Serves 4

1 (4-serving) package JELL-O sugar-free vanilla cook-and-serve
   pudding mix
1 (4-serving) package JELL-O sugar-free strawberry gelatin
¾ cup water
3 cups frozen unsweetened strawberries, thawed, and undrained
1 tablespoon lemon juice
1 teaspoon rum extract
2 cups Wells' Blue Bunny sugar- and fat-free vanilla ice cream

In a medium saucepan, combine dry pudding mix, dry gelatin, and water. Stir in undrained strawberries. Cook over medium heat until mixture thickens and starts to boil, stirring often, being careful not to crush the strawberries. Stir in lemon juice and rum extract. Place saucepan on a wire rack and allow to cool for 5 minutes. For each serving, place ½ cup ice cream in a sundae dish and spoon about ⅓ cup warm sauce over top.

Each serving equals:

DIABETIC EXCHANGES: 1 Starch/Carbohydrate •
½ Fruit or 1½ Starch/Carbohydrate

152 Calories • 0 gm Fat • 6 gm Protein •
32 gm Carbohydrate • 221 mg Sodium •
136 mg Calcium • 2 gm Fiber

HE: ¾ Fruit • 1 Slider • 10 Optional Calories

Easy Tiramisu

The original of this romantic and pretty Italian-inspired dessert is made with sugary ladyfingers, but I think sponge cake is even tastier and soaks up all the creamy filling even better!

🔘 Serves 6

> 1 (4-serving) package sponge shortcakes
> ¾ cup plain fat-free yogurt
> ⅓ cup Carnation Nonfat Dry Milk Powder
> ½ cup + 1 tablespoon Splenda Granular ☆
> 1 (8-ounce) package Philadelphia fat-free cream cheese
> ¾ cup Cool Whip Free
> 1 (4-serving) package JELL-O sugar-free instant vanilla pudding mix
> 1½ cups cold water
> ⅔ cup hot water
> 1 tablespoon instant coffee crystals
> 1 teaspoon brandy extract
> ½ teaspoon unsweetened cocoa

Cut sponge cakes in half. Evenly arrange bottom halves in an 8-by-8-inch baking dish. Set aside. In a medium bowl, combine yogurt and dry milk powder. Gently stir in ¼ cup Splenda and Cool Whip Free. Set aside. In a large bowl, stir cream cheese with a spoon until soft. Fold in ¼ cup Splenda and 1 cup of yogurt mixture. In a medium bowl, combine dry pudding mix and cold water. Mix well using a wire whisk. Add pudding mixture to cream cheese mixture. Mix gently to combine. In a small bowl, combine hot water, coffee crystals, remaining 1 tablespoon Splenda, and brandy extract. Drizzle half of coffee mixture over sponge cake halves. Spread half of cream cheese mixture over top. Repeat layers, spread remaining yogurt mixture over top. Evenly sprinkle top with cocoa. Cover and refrigerate for at least 2 hours. Cut into 6 servings.

HINT: Substitute 1 (4-serving) package sugar-free raspberry gelatin for coffee crystals for a whole new taste.

Each serving equals:

DIABETIC EXCHANGES: 1½ Starch/Carbohydrate •
½ Meat

---

157 Calories • 1 gm Fat • 10 gm Protein •
27 gm Carbohydrate • 580 mg Sodium •
117 mg Calcium • 1 gm Fiber

HE: ⅔ Protein • ⅔ Bread • ⅓ Fat Free Milk •
¼ Slider • 12 Optional Calories

Cherry Pretzel Torte

Yes, I know this sounds a little strange, but something magical occurs when you make a crust out of everyone's favorite salty snack food, then top it with rich layers of fruit and creamy goodness. Sometimes the most wonderful things in life are the most unexpected! (My son James, the cherry lover in the family, thought this was a real winner.) ☻ Serves 8

2¼ cups crushed reduced-sodium pretzels ☆
¼ cup Splenda Granular ☆
2 tablespoons + 2 teaspoons I Can't Believe It's Not Butter! Light margarine, melted
1 (4-serving) package JELL-O sugar-free vanilla cook-and-serve pudding mix
1 (4-serving) package JELL-O sugar-free cherry gelatin
1 (16-ounce) can tart red cherries, packed in water, undrained
¾ cup water
1 (8-ounce) package Philadelphia fat-free cream cheese
¾ cup plain fat-free yogurt
⅓ cup Carnation Nonfat Dry Milk Powder
1 teaspoon vanilla extract
1 cup Cool Whip Lite

Preheat oven to 350 degrees. Spray a 9-by-13-inch cake pan with butter-flavored cooking spray. In a large bowl, combine 2 cups pretzels, 2 tablespoons Splenda, and melted margarine. Press mixture into prepared cake pan. Bake for 15 minutes. Meanwhile, in a medium saucepan, combine dry pudding mix, dry gelatin, undrained cherries, and water. Cook over medium heat until mixture thickens and starts to boil, stirring often, being careful not to crush the cherries. Place cake pan and saucepan on wire racks and allow to cool completely. In a large bowl, stir cream cheese with a spoon until soft. Add yogurt and dry milk powder. Mix well to combine. Fold in remaining 2 tablespoons Splenda, vanilla extract, and Cool Whip Lite. Spread cream cheese mixture over cooled pretzel crust. Spoon cooled cherry mixture over cream cheese mixture and top with remaining ¼ cup crushed pretzels. Refrigerate for at least 2 hours. Cut into 8 servings.

HINT: A self-seal sandwich bag works great for crushing pretzels.

Each serving equals:

DIABETIC EXCHANGES: 1½ Starch/Carbohydrate •
½ Fat • ½ Meat • ½ Fruit

---

171 Calories • 3 gm Fat • 9 gm Protein •
27 gm Carbohydrate • 582 mg Sodium •
89 mg Calcium • 1 gm Fiber

HE: ¾ Bread • ½ Fat • ½ Protein • ½ Fruit •
¼ Fat Free Milk • ¼ Slider • 18 Optional Calories

Rhubarb Pizza Dessert

Can't you just hear the cheers when you carry this into the dining room, and your assembled family members go wild? The rosy-red color makes it oh-so-festive, and the mouthwatering sweet-tart taste of the rhubarb warms the heart as much as it pleases the tummy! If you want to know what summer in Iowa tastes like, this is it!

◔ Serves 12

> 1 (8-ounce) can Pillsbury Reduced Fat Crescent Rolls
> 1 (4-serving) package JELL-O sugar-free vanilla cook-and-serve pudding mix
> 1 (4-serving) package JELL-O sugar-free strawberry gelatin
> 1 cup water
> 2 cups finely chopped fresh or frozen rhubarb
> 1 (8-ounce) package Philadelphia fat-free cream cheese
> ¾ cup Cool Whip Lite

Preheat oven to 425 degrees. Pat crescent rolls into a 10-by-15-inch rimmed baking pan, being sure to seal perforations. Bake for 6 to 7 minutes or until golden brown. Place baking pan on a wire rack and allow to cool completely. In a medium saucepan, combine dry pudding mix, dry gelatin, and water. Stir in rhubarb. Cook over medium heat until mixture thickens and rhubarb becomes soft, stirring constantly. Remove from heat. Stir in cream cheese. Mix well using a wire whisk until blended. Spread mixture evenly over crust. Refrigerate for 1 hour. Evenly drop Cool Whip Lite by tablespoons to form 12 mounds. Cut into 12 servings.

Each serving equals:

DIABETIC EXCHANGES: 1 Starch/Carbohydrate • ½ Fat

108 Calories • 4 gm Fat • 5 gm Protein •
13 gm Carbohydrate • 326 mg Sodium •
18 mg Calcium • 0 gm Fiber

HE: ⅔ Bread • ⅓ Protein • ⅓ Vegetable • ¼ Slider

Apple Dumpling Dessert

Nothing could be more homey or soothing than this warm apple confection that's a true American classic! If you didn't grow up with a grandma who treated you to such sweet and soothing delights, you've got a wonderfully cozy adventure in store. If a dish like this recalls your favorite memories, then here they come again!

◎ Serves 6

1 (7.5 ounce) can Pillsbury refrigerated buttermilk biscuits

2 cups (4 small) cored, unpeeled, and thinly sliced cooking apples

⅔ cup Carnation Nonfat Dry Milk Powder

½ cup water

½ cup Splenda Granular

½ cup Log Cabin Sugar Free Maple Syrup

2 tablespoons I Can't Believe It's Not Butter! Light margarine

Preheat oven to 375 degrees. Spray an 8-by-8-inch baking dish with butter-flavored cooking spray. Separate biscuits and place in prepared baking dish. Layer apple slices evenly over biscuits. In a small saucepan, combine dry milk powder and water. Add Splenda, maple syrup, and margarine. Cook over medium heat until mixture starts to boil, stirring constantly. Pour hot syrup mixture over apples. Bake for 35 to 45 minutes or until apples are tender and biscuits are done in center. Serve warm.

HINT: Good topped with 1 tablespoon Cool Whip Lite or ¼ cup Wells' Blue Bunny sugar- and fat-free vanilla ice cream, but don't forget to count the few additional calories.

Each serving equals:

DIABETIC EXCHANGES: 1 Starch/Carbohydrate • 1 Fruit • ½ Fat

154 Calories • 2 gm Fat • 5 gm Protein • 29 gm Carbohydrate • 408 mg Sodium • 95 mg Calcium • 2 gm Fiber

HE: 1¼ Bread • ⅔ Fruit • ½ Fat • ⅓ Fat Free Milk • ¼ Slider • 1 Optional Calorie

Apple Lasagna Dessert

This is a takeoff of sorts on an old Eastern European tradition called noodle pudding, a sweet pasta dish. But by adding apples to the blend, I've created an all-American version that looks and tastes spectacular. ☻ Serves 8

> 1 (4-serving) package JELL-O sugar-free vanilla cook-and-serve pudding mix
> 1 cup unsweetened apple juice
> 3 cups (6 small) cored, peeled, and sliced cooking apples
> ¾ cup shredded Kraft reduced-fat Cheddar cheese
> 1 (8-ounce) package Philadelphia fat-free cream cheese
> ½ teaspoon vanilla extract
> ½ cup Splenda Granular ☆
> 6 cooked lasagna noodles, rinsed and drained ☆
> 3 tablespoons all-purpose flour
> ¼ cup quick oats
> 1 teaspoon apple pie spice
> 1 tablespoon + 1 teaspoon I Can't Believe It's Not Butter! Light margarine
> ½ cup Cool Whip Lite

Preheat oven to 350 degrees. Spray an 8-by-8-inch baking dish with butter-flavored cooking spray. In a medium saucepan, combine dry pudding mix and apple juice. Stir in apples. Cook over medium heat until mixture thickens and apples become soft, stirring often. Place saucepan on a wire rack and allow to cool for 10 minutes. Meanwhile in a medium bowl, combine Cheddar cheese, cream cheese, vanilla extract, and 2 tablespoons Splenda. Spoon 1 cup apple mixture into bottom of prepared baking dish. Arrange 3 noodles evenly over apples. Spread cheese mixture over noodles. Top with remaining 3 noodles and remaining apple mixture. In a small bowl, combine flour, oats, apple pie spice, and remaining 6 tablespoons Splenda. Stir in margarine until mixture is crumbly. Evenly sprinkle mixture over top. Bake for 50 minutes.

Place baking dish on a wire rack and allow to cool for 15 minutes. Cut into 8 servings. When serving, top each piece with 1 tablespoon Cool Whip Lite.

Each serving equals:

DIABETIC EXCHANGES: 1 Starch/Carbohydrate • 1 Fruit • 1 Meat • ½ Fat

214 Calories • 6 gm Fat • 9 gm Protein • 31 gm Carbohydrate • 196 mg Sodium • 163 mg Calcium • 2 gm Fiber

HE: 1 Bread • 1 Fruit • 1 Protein • ¼ Fat • ¼ Slider • 6 Optional Calories

Strawberry Chocolate Truffle Pizza

My dessert pizzas have won me new friends from all over the country, and I couldn't be more pleased that they appeal to kids as much as they do adults! ☻ Serves 12

> 1 (8-ounce) can Pillsbury Reduced Fat Crescent Rolls
> 1 (8-ounce) package Philadelphia fat-free cream cheese
> 2 tablespoons Splenda Granular
> 1½ teaspoons almond extract ☆
> ½ cup chopped almonds
> 2 (4-serving) packages JELL-O sugar-free instant chocolate fudge
>   pudding mix
> ⅔ cup Carnation Nonfat Dry Milk Powder
> 1½ cups plain fat-free yogurt
> 1 cup water
> ¾ cup Cool Whip Free
> 4 cups fresh whole strawberries

Preheat oven to 400 degrees. Pat crescent rolls into a 9-by-12-inch rimmed baking sheet sprayed with butter-flavored cooking spray. Gently press dough to cover bottom of pan, being sure to seal perforations. Bake for 6 to 7 minutes. Place baking sheet on a wire rack and allow to cool. In a medium bowl, stir cream cheese with a spoon until soft. Add Splenda and ½ teaspoon almond extract. Mix well to combine. Stir in almonds. Spread mixture evenly over cooled crust. In a large bowl, combine dry pudding mix and dry milk powder. Add yogurt and water. Mix well using a wire whisk. Fold in remaining 1 teaspoon almond extract and Cool Whip Free. Evenly spread chocolate mixture over cream cheese mixture. Cut strawberries in half lengthwise. Attractively place strawberries, cut-side down, in chocolate mixture. Refrigerate for at least 30 minutes. Cut into 12 servings.

HINT: Do not use inexpensive rolls as they don't cover the pan properly.

Each serving equals:

DIABETIC EXCHANGES: 1½ Starch/Carbohydrate •
1 Fat • ½ Meat

---

190 Calories • 6 gm Fat • 9 gm Protein •
25 gm Carbohydrate • 534 mg Sodium •
124 mg Calcium • 1 gm Fiber

HE: ⅔ Bread • ½ Protein • ⅓ Fat Free Milk • ⅓ Fat •
⅓ Fruit • ¼ Slider • 12 Optional Calories

Strawberry Almond Crepes

Now don't get the idea that this is some kind of gourmet recipe, because after all, crepes are just skinny pancakes! Of course, the cream cheese filling is scrumptious enough to be served in a big-city restaurant . . . but you can enjoy it at home whenever you like!

◐ Serves 4

> 2 cups sliced fresh strawberries
> ½ cup Splenda Granular ☆
> 1 cup Aunt Jemima Reduced-Calorie
>   Pancake Mix
> 1 cup water
> 2 eggs or equivalent in egg substitute
> 1 (8-ounce) package Philadelphia fat-free
>   cream cheese
> 1 teaspoon almond extract
> ½ cup Cool Whip Free
> 2 tablespoons slivered almonds

In a small bowl, combine strawberries and ¼ cup Splenda, and set aside. In a medium bowl, combine pancake mix, 2 tablespoons Splenda, water, and eggs. Mix well using a wire whisk until blended. Heat an 8-inch skillet and lightly spray with butter-flavored cooking spray. Pour ¼ cup batter into hot skillet, immediately tilting pan until batter covers bottom. Cook until edges start to dry and center is set. Quickly flip over and lightly brown other side. Place on plate and set aside. Repeat process until all 8 crepes have been prepared. In a medium bowl, stir cream cheese with a spoon until soft. Stir in remaining 2 tablespoons Splenda, almond extract, and Cool Whip Free. Spoon about 2 tablespoons cream cheese mixture on each crepe and roll up. For each serving, place 2 crepes seam side down on a dessert plate, spoon ½ cup strawberries over crepes, and sprinkle 1½ teaspoons almonds over the top.

Each serving equals:

DIABETIC EXCHANGES: 1½ Starch/Carbohydrate •
1½ Meat • ½ Fruit

---

262 Calories • 6 gm Fat • 18 gm Protein •
34 gm Carbohydrate • 764 mg Sodium •
215 mg Calcium • 5 gm Fiber

HE: 1½ Protein • 1⅓ Bread • ½ Fruit • ¼ Fat •
¼ Slider • 16 Optional Calories

Lemon Paradise Muffins

Finding those luscious little bits of fruit inside these delicate muffins is just part of the fun! And yes, I couldn't resist including my favorite pecans, too. Homemade muffins are so much healthier than the kind you can buy in the store, you'll be doing yourself and your family a favor if you put them on the menu.

● Serves 8

⅔ cup Carnation Nonfat Dry Milk Powder
1 cup water
1 teaspoon white vinegar
1½ cups all-purpose flour
1 (4-serving) package JELL-O sugar-free instant vanilla
    pudding mix
1 (4-serving) package JELL-O sugar-free lemon gelatin
1 teaspoon baking powder
½ teaspoon baking soda
¼ cup chopped pecans
1 (8-ounce) can crushed pineapple, packed in fruit juice,
    undrained

Preheat oven to 375 degrees. Spray 8 wells of a 12-hole muffin pan with butter-flavored cooking spray or line with paper liners. In a small bowl, combine dry milk powder, water, and vinegar. Set aside. In a large bowl, combine flour, dry pudding mix, dry gelatin, baking powder, baking soda, and pecans. Add undrained pineapple and milk mixture. Mix gently just to combine. Evenly spoon batter into prepared muffin wells. Bake for 16 to 18 minutes or until a toothpick inserted in center comes out clean. Place muffin pan on a wire rack and allow to cool for 5 minutes. Remove muffins from pan and continue cooling on wire rack.

HINT: Fill unused muffin wells with water. It protects the muffin
    pan and ensures even baking.

Each serving equals:

DIABETIC EXCHANGES: 1½ Starch/Carbohydrate • ½ Fat

167 Calories • 3 gm Fat • 5 gm Protein •
30 gm Carbohydrate • 363 mg Sodium •
112 mg Calcium • 1 gm Fiber

HE: 1 Bread • ½ Fat • ¼ Fat Free Milk • ¼ Fruit •
18 Optional Calories

Peanut Butter and Jelly Muffins

These kid-pleasers (and husband-pleasers) are delectable for breakfast, but because they also freeze beautifully, they're wonderful for after-school snacks, late-night nibbling, and just about anytime at all. I've suggested grape for the "jelly" part, but feel free to experiment with any flavor spreadable fruit that you enjoy!

◐ Serves 8

> 1½ cups all-purpose flour
> 1½ teaspoons baking powder
> ½ teaspoon baking soda
> ¼ cup Splenda Granular
> 1 (4-serving) package JELL-O sugar-free instant vanilla pudding mix
> ¼ cup Peter Pan reduced-fat peanut butter
> 1 egg or equivalent in egg substitute
> ½ cup unsweetened applesauce
> ½ fat free milk
> 3 tablespoons grape spreadable fruit

Preheat oven to 400 degrees. Spray 8 wells of a 12-hole muffin pan with butter-flavored cooking spray or line with paper liners. In a large bowl, combine flour, baking powder, baking soda, Splenda, and dry pudding mix. Add peanut butter. Mix until crumbly. In a small bowl, combine egg, applesauce, and milk. Add to flour mixture. Mix just until combined. Fill muffin wells ⅓ full with batter. Place about ¾ teaspoon spreadable fruit on top of each. Cover with remaining batter. Bake for 18 to 20 minutes or until a toothpick inserted in center comes out clean. Place muffin pan on a wire rack and allow to cool for 5 minutes. Remove muffins from pan and continue cooling on wire rack.

HINT: Fill unused muffin wells with water. It protects the muffin pan and ensures even baking.

Each serving equals:

DIABETIC EXCHANGES: 1½ Starch/Carbohydrate •
½ Meat • ½ Fruit

---

180 Calories • 4 gm Fat • 5 gm Protein •
31 gm Carbohydrate • 389 mg Sodium •
77 mg Calcium • 1 gm Fiber

HE: 1 Bread • ⅔ Protein • ½ Fat • ½ Fruit •
¼ Slider • 1 Optional Calorie

Sunshine Line
Cherry Chocolate Muffins

Sweet desserts have always sent sunshine pouring into my life—how about yours? These little gems have lots of goodies hidden inside, a veritable treasure chest of flavor in one perfect package. Have fun with these! ☻ Serves 8

⅔ cup Carnation Nonfat Dry
    Milk Powder
½ cup water
2 teaspoons white vinegar
1½ cups all-purpose flour
1 (4-serving) package JELL-O
    sugar-free instant vanilla
    pudding mix
1½ teaspoons baking powder
½ teaspoon baking soda
2 tablespoons mini chocolate
    chips

¼ cup chopped pecans
1 egg, slightly beaten, or
    equivalent in egg
    substitute
1 (8-ounce) can crushed
    pineapple, packed in fruit
    juice, undrained
1 teaspoon almond extract
12 maraschino cherries,
    chopped

Preheat oven to 350 degrees. Spray 8 wells of a 12-hole muffin pan with butter-flavored cooking spray or line with paper liners. In a small bowl, combine dry milk powder, water, and vinegar. Set aside. In a large bowl, combine flour, dry pudding mix, baking powder, and baking soda. Stir in chocolate chips and pecans. Stir egg, undrained pineapple, almond extract, and maraschino cherries into milk mixture. Add milk mixture to flour mixture. Mix gently to combine. Evenly spoon batter into prepared muffin wells. Bake for 22 to 25 minutes or until a toothpick inserted in center comes out clean. Place muffin pan on a wire rack and allow to cool for 5 minutes. Remove muffins from pan and continue cooling on wire rack.

HINT: Fill unused muffin wells with water. It protects the muffin
       pan and ensures even baking.

Each serving equals:

DIABETIC EXCHANGES: 2 Starch/Carbohydrate • ½ Fat

200 Calories • 4 gm Fat • 6 gm Protein •
35 gm Carbohydrate • 375 mg Sodium •
133 mg Calcium • 1 gm Fiber

HE: 1 Bread • ½ Fat • ¼ Fruit • ¼ Fat Free Milk •
½ Slider • 4 Optional Calories

Carrot Raisin Cake Muffins

These cousins of carrot cake are a delightful accompaniment when you're serving a festive brunch of omelets, and they're sturdy enough to pack in a lunchbox or brown bag to take to school or work. It's nice to know that you're getting a few extra bites of vegetable in, too! ☺ Serves 8

1½ cups all-purpose flour
1 (4-serving) package JELL-O
    sugar-free instant vanilla
    pudding mix
1 teaspoon baking powder
½ teaspoon baking soda
1 teaspoon apple pie spice
1 cup finely grated carrots
½ cup raisins

2 tablespoons chopped pecans
⅓ cup plain fat-free yogurt
2 tablespoons Kraft fat-free
    mayonnaise
⅓ cup fat-free milk
2 eggs or equivalent in egg
    substitute
1 teaspoon vanilla extract

Preheat oven to 350 degrees. Spray 8 holes of a 12-hole muffin pan with butter-flavored cooking spray, or line with paper liners. In a large bowl, combine flour, dry pudding mix, baking powder, baking soda, and apple pie spice. Stir in carrots, raisins, and pecans. In a medium bowl, combine yogurt and mayonnaise. Add milk, eggs, and vanilla extract. Mix well to combine. Add yogurt mixture to flour mixture. Mix gently just to combine. Evenly spoon batter into prepared muffin cups, filling each about ⅔ full. Bake for 20 to 23 minutes or until a toothpick inserted in center comes out clean. Place muffin pan on a wire rack and cool for 5 minutes. Remove muffins from pan and continue cooling on wire rack.

HINT: Fill unused muffin wells with water. It protects the muffin
       pan and ensures even baking.

Each serving equals:

DIABETIC EXCHANGES: 1½ Starch/Carbohydrate •
½ Fruit • ½ Fat

---

175 Calories • 3 gm Fat • 5 gm Protein •
32 gm Carbohydrate • 372 mg Sodium •
83 mg Calcium • 2 gm Fiber

HE: 1 Bread • ½ Fruit • ¼ Vegetable • ¼ Fat •
¼ Protein • ¼ Slider • 3 Optional Calories

Carrot Pineapple Bread

This is one of the moistest and most flavorful breads I've ever created, and you can thank everything from the carrots to the applesauce to the pineapple for that! What's great about this recipe (and many of the others) is that they freeze really well, reheat beautifully, and make wonderful holiday gifts. ☻ Serves 8

1½ cups all-purpose flour
½ cup Splenda Granular
1 (4-serving) package JELL-O
    sugar-free instant vanilla
    pudding mix
1 teaspoon baking powder
½ teaspoon baking soda
1 teaspoon apple pie spice
1 cup unsweetened applesauce

1 teaspoon vanilla extract
1 egg or equivalent in egg
    substitute
1 (8-ounce) can crushed
    pineapple, packed in fruit
    juice, undrained
1 cup shredded carrots
¼ cup chopped walnuts

Preheat oven to 350 degrees. Spray a 9-by-5-inch loaf pan with butter-flavored cooking spray. In a large bowl, combine flour, Splenda, dry pudding mix, baking powder, baking soda, and apple pie spice. In a small bowl, combine applesauce, vanilla extract, egg, and undrained pineapple. Add applesauce mixture to flour mixture. Mix just until combined. Fold in carrots and walnuts. Pour mixture into prepared loaf pan. Bake for 50 to 55 minutes or until a toothpick inserted in center comes out clean. Place loaf pan on a wire rack and cool for 5 minutes. Remove from pan and continue cooling on wire rack. Cut into 8 servings.

Each serving equals:

DIABETIC EXCHANGES: 1½ Starch/Carbohydrate •
½ Fruit

167 Calories • 3 gm Fat • 4 gm Protein •
31 gm Carbohydrate • 319 mg Sodium •
53 mg Calcium • 2 gm Fiber

HE: 1 Bread • ½ Fruit • ¼ Vegetable • ¼ Protein •
¼ Fat • 19 Optional Calories

Holiday Pumpkin Pancakes with Maple Cream

My grandbabies love pancakes for breakfast, so when the boys are visiting Cliff and me, I often get up early to fix them something special. This recipe takes very little work, but you've never seen smiles like the ones you'll get when you slide these gorgeous, golden circles onto a plate. And one lick of the maple cream will get you a great big kiss! ☻ Serves 8 (2 each)

1 (8-ounce) package
   Philadelphia fat-free
   cream cheese
3/4 cup Log Cabin Sugar Free
   Maple Syrup
1 1/2 cups Bisquick Reduced-Fat
   Baking Mix
1 teaspoon pumpkin pie spice

2 tablespoons Splenda Granular
1/2 cup raisins
1/4 cup chopped walnuts
1 (15-ounce) can solid-packed
   pumpkin
1 egg, beaten, or equivalent in
   egg substitute

In a medium bowl, stir cream cheese with a spoon until soft. Add maple syrup. Mix well to combine. Set aside. In a large bowl, combine baking mix, pumpkin pie spice, Splenda, raisins, and walnuts. Add pumpkin and egg. Mix well to combine. Using a 1/4-cup measure as a guide, pour batter on griddle or in a large skillet sprayed with butter-flavored cooking spray to form sixteen pancakes. Brown lightly on both sides. For each serving, place two pancakes on a plate and spoon maple cream over top.

Each serving equals:

DIABETIC EXCHANGES: 1 1/2 Starch/Carbohydrate •
1 Meat • 1/2 Fruit • 1/2 Fat

---

200 Calories • 4 gm Fat • 8 gm Protein •
33 mg Carbohydrate • 494 mg Sodium •
47 mg Calcium • 3 gm Fiber

HE: 1 Bread • 3/4 Protein • 1/2 Vegetable • 1/2 Fruit •
1/4 Fat • 16 Optional Calories

Southern Banana Praline Muffins

Sometimes a recipe called "praline" has a nut topping, but here I've stirred the sweet and nutty ingredients right into the batter. Talk about your Southern hospitality—serve these to your guests and you'll always have more company than you know what to do with!

○ Serves 8

1½ cups Bisquick Reduced-Fat
    Baking Mix
¼ cup chopped pecans
½ cup Splenda Granular ☆
⅔ cup (2 medium) mashed
    ripe bananas

1 egg or equivalent in egg
    substitute
⅓ cup unsweetened applesauce
1 teaspoon vanilla extract

Preheat oven to 400 degrees. Spray eight wells of a 12-hole muffin pan with butter-flavored cooking spray or line with paper liners. In a large bowl, combine baking mix, pecans and Splenda. In a small bowl, combine mashed bananas, egg, applesauce, and vanilla extract. Add banana mixture to baking mix mixture. Mix gently just to combine. Evenly spoon batter into prepared muffin wells. Bake for 15 to 18 minutes or until a toothpick inserted in the center comes out clean. Place muffin pan on a wire rack and allow to cool for 10 minutes. Remove muffins from pan and continue cooling on wire rack.

HINT: Fill unused muffin wells with water. It protects the muffin pan and ensures even baking.

Each serving equals:

DIABETIC EXCHANGES: 1½ Starch/Carbohydrate •
½ Fruit • ½ Fat or 2 Starch/Carbohydrate • ½ Fat

137 Calories • 5 gm Fat • 3 gm Protein •
20 gm Carbohydrate • 270 mg Sodium •
24 mg Calcium • 1 gm Fiber

HE: 1 Bread • ½ Fruit • ½ Fat • 17 Optional Calories

Heavenly Banana Bread

Every angel-in-training should have at least one irresistible quick bread ready to whip up at a moment's notice! Oh, sure, you could settle for a standard banana bread blend, but the philosophy of Healthy Exchanges rests on treating yourself well. Anyone who tastes a slice of this exceptional bread will think it's the answer to a prayer!   ♥   Serves 8

½ cup plain fat-free yogurt
⅓ cup Kraft fat-free
   mayonnaise
1 egg, beaten, or equivalent in
   egg substitute
⅔ cup (2 medium) mashed
   ripe bananas
1½ cups all-purpose flour

1 (4-serving) package JELL-O
   sugar-free instant banana
   cream pudding mix
½ teaspoon baking soda
1 teaspoon baking powder
¼ cup chopped pecans
2 tablespoons mini chocolate
   chips

Preheat oven to 350 degrees. Spray a 9-by-5-inch loaf pan with butter-flavored cooking spray. In a large bowl, combine yogurt, mayonnaise, egg, and mashed bananas. Add flour, dry pudding mix, baking soda, and baking powder. Mix just to combine. Fold in pecans and chocolate chips. Pour batter into prepared loaf pan. Bake for 1 hour or until a toothpick inserted in center comes out clean. Place loaf pan on a wire rack and cool in pan for 5 minutes. Remove from pan and continue cooling on wire rack. Cut into 8 servings.

Each serving equals:

DIABETIC EXCHANGES: 1½ Starch/Carbohydrate •
½ Fruit • ½ Fat

208 Calories • 4 gm Fat • 5 gm Protein •
38 gm Carbohydrate • 494 mg Sodium •
74 mg Calcium • 2 gm Fiber

HE: 1 Bread • ½ Fruit • ½ Fat • ½ Slider •
4 Optional Calories

Apricot Walnut Bread

The technique I use to "rehydrate" the dried apricots in this recipe will also work for other dried fruits, so put on your creativity cap and think of other recipes that might benefit from the addition of healthy fruit. This bread is both pretty and very tasty, making it a great choice for an office party or committee meeting.

● Serves 8 (1 thick or 2 thin slices)

½ cup chopped dried apricots
¾ cup boiling water
1½ cups all-purpose flour
1 (4-serving) package JELL-O sugar-free instant vanilla pudding
    mix
1 teaspoon baking soda
1 teaspoon baking powder
½ cup Splenda Granular
1 egg or equivalent in egg substitute
1 tablespoon + 1 teaspoon I Can't Believe It's Not Butter! Light
    margarine, melted
¼ cup fat-free milk
1 teaspoon vanilla extract
¼ cup chopped walnuts

Preheat oven to 350 degrees. Spray a 9-by-5-inch loaf pan with butter-flavored cooking spray. In a medium bowl, combine apricots and boiling water. Let set for 1 hour. Drain and reserve liquid. In a large bowl, combine flour, dry pudding mix, baking soda, baking powder, and Splenda. In a small bowl, beat egg with a fork. Add margarine, ½ cup reserved apricot liquid, skim milk, and vanilla extract. Add egg mixture to flour mixture. Mix just to combine. Stir in apricots and walnuts. Spoon mixture into prepared loaf pan. Bake for 35 to 40 minutes or until a toothpick inserted in center comes out clean. Place loaf pan on a wire rack and let set for 10 minutes. Remove bread from pan and continue cooling on wire rack. Cut into 8 thick or 16 thin slices.

Each serving equals:

DIABETIC EXCHANGES: 1 Starch • ½ Fruit • ½ Fat

151 Calories • 3 gm Fat • 4 gm Protein •
27 gm Carbohydrate • 406 mg Sodium •
57 mg Calcium • 2 gm Fiber

HE: 1 Bread • ½ Fruit • ½ Fat • ¼ Protein •
¼ Slider • 1 Optional Calorie

Holiday Cranberry Bread

One of the reasons I enjoy baking with cranberries is those glorious bursts of RED that peep out every time you cut a slice! I know you'll agree this fruity confection belongs on every buffet table at your house from Halloween to New Year's. Who knows, it may become one of your signature festive desserts.

● Serves 8 (1 thick or 2 thin slices)

> 1½ cups all-purpose flour
> 1 teaspoon baking powder
> ½ teaspoon baking soda
> ¼ cup Splenda Granular
> 1 (4-serving) package JELL-O sugar-free instant vanilla
>   pudding mix
> 1 cup coarsely chopped fresh or frozen
>   cranberries
> ¼ cup chopped walnuts
> ½ cup unsweetened orange juice
> ⅓ cup unsweetened applesauce
> 1 egg or equivalent in egg substitute
> 1 teaspoon vanilla extract

Preheat oven to 350 degrees. Spray a 9-by-5-inch loaf pan with butter-flavored cooking spray. In a large bowl, combine flour, baking powder, baking soda, Splenda, and dry pudding mix. Stir in cranberries and walnuts. In a small bowl, combine orange juice, applesauce, egg, and vanilla extract. Add orange juice mixture to flour mixture. Mix well to combine. Pour batter into prepared loaf pan. Bake for 50 to 60 minutes or until a toothpick inserted in center comes out clean. Place loaf pan on a wire rack and cool for 10 minutes. Remove from pan and continue to cool completely on wire rack. Cut into 8 thick or 16 thin slices.

Each serving equals:

DIABETIC EXCHANGES: 1½ Starch/Carbohydrate •
½ Fruit

147 Calories • 3 gm Fat • 4 gm Protein •
26 gm Carbohydrate • 393 mg Sodium •
46 mg Calcium • 1 gm Fiber

HE: 1 Bread • ½ Fruit • ¼ Fat • ¼ Protein •
18 Optional Calories

Index

I want to hear from you . . .

Besides my family, the love of my life is creating "common folk" healthy recipes and solving everyday cooking questions in *The Healthy Exchanges Way*. Everyone who uses my recipes is considered part of the Healthy Exchanges Family, so please write to me if you have any questions, comments, or suggestions. I will do my best to answer. With your support, I'll continue to stir up even more recipes and cooking tips for the Family in the years to come.

Write to: JoAnna M. Lund
              c/o Healthy Exchanges, Inc.
              P.O. Box 80
              DeWitt, IA 52742

If you prefer, you can fax me at 1-563-659-2126 or contact me via E-mail by writing to HealthyJo@aol.com. Or visit my Healthy Exchanges Internet Web site at: http://www.healthyexchanges.com.

Ever since I began stirring up Healthy Exchanges recipes, I wanted every dish to be rich in flavor and lively in taste. As part of my pursuit of satisfying eating and healthy living for a lifetime, I decided to create my own line of spices.

JO'S SPICES

. . . A Healthy Way to Spice Up Your Life™

JO's Spices are salt-, sugar-, wheat-, and MSG-free, and you can substitute them in any of the recipes calling for traditional spice mixes. If you're interested in hearing more about my special blends, please call Healthy Exchanges at 1-563-659-8234 for more information or to order. If you prefer, write to JO's Spices, c/o Healthy Exchanges, P.O. Box 80, DeWitt, IA 52742.

Now That You've Seen
The Healthy Exchanges
Diabetic Desserts Cookbook,
Why Not Order
The Healthy Exchanges Food Newsletter?

If you enjoyed the recipes in this cookbook and would like to cook up even more of these "common folk" healthy dishes, you may want to subscribe to *The Healthy Exchanges Food Newsletter*.

This monthly 12-page newsletter contains 30-plus new recipes *every month* in such columns as:

- Reader Exchange
- Reader Requests
- Recipe Makeover
- Micro Corner
- Dinner for Two

- Crock Pot Luck
- Meatless Main Dishes
- Rise & Shine
- Our Small World

- Brown Bagging It
- Snack Attack
- Side Dishes
- Main Dishes
- Desserts

In addition to all the recipes, other regular features include:

- The Editor's Motivational Corner
- Dining Out Question & Answer
- Cooking Question & Answer
- New Product Alert
- Success Profiles of Winners in the Losing Game
- Exercise Advice from a Cardiac Rehab Specialist
- Nutrition Advice from a Registered Dietitian
- Positive Thought for the Month

Just as in this cookbook, all *Healthy Exchanges Food Newsletter* recipes are calculated in three distinct ways: 1) Weight Loss Choices, 2) Calories with Fat and Fiber Grams, and 3) Diabetic Exchanges.

The cost for a one-year (12-issue) subscription is $28.50. To order, simply complete the form and mail to us *or* call our toll-free number. We accept all major credit cards.

_____ Yes, I want to subscribe to *The Healthy Exchanges Food Newsletter*. $28.50 Yearly Subscription Cost with Storage Binder $_____

_____ $22.50 Yearly Subscription Cost without Binder . . . . $_____

_____ Foreign orders please add $6.00 for money exchange and extra postage. . . . . $_____

_____ I'm not sure, so please send me a sample copy at $3.50 . . . . $_____

Please make check payable to HEALTHY EXCHANGES or pay by VISA, MasterCard, Discover, or American Express

CARD NUMBER: _____   EXPIRATION DATE: _____

SIGNATURE: _____

Signature required for all credit card orders.

Or Order Toll-Free, using your credit card, at 1-800-766-8961

NAME:_____

ADDRESS:_____

CITY: _____   STATE: _____   ZIP: _____

TELEPHONE:(   ) _____

If additional orders for the newsletter are to be sent to an address other than the one listed above, please use a separate sheet and attach to this form.

MAIL TO: **HEALTHY EXCHANGES**
             P.O. BOX 80
             DeWitt, IA 52742-0124

             1-800-766-8961 for Customer Orders
             1-563-659-8234 for Customer Service

Thank you for your order, and for choosing to become a part of the Healthy Exchanges Family!

About the Author

JoAnna M. Lund, a graduate of the University of Western Illinois, worked as a commercial insurance underwriter for eighteen years before starting her own business, Healthy Exchanges, Inc., which publishes cookbooks, a monthly newsletter, motivational booklets, and inspirational audiotapes. Healthy Exchanges Cookbooks have more than 1 million copies in print. A popular speaker with hospitals, support groups for heart patients and diabetics, and service and volunteer organizations, she has appeared on QVC, on hundreds of regional television and radio shows, and has been featured in newspapers and magazines across the country.

The recipient of numerous business awards, JoAnna was an Iowa delegate to the national White House Conference on Small Business. She is a member of the International Association of Culinary Professionals, the Society for Nutritional Education, and other professional publishing and marketing associations. She lives with her husband, Clifford, in DeWitt, Iowa.

Healthy Exchanges recipes are a great way to begin—
but if your goal is living healthy for a lifetime,

You Need **HELP!**

JoAnna M. Lund's
Healthy Exchanges Lifetime Plan

"I lost 130 pounds and reclaimed my health by following a
Four Part Plan that emphasizes not only Healthy Eating, but
also Moderate Exercise, Lifestyle Changes and Goal-setting,
and most important of all, Positive Attitude."

- If you've lost weight before but failed to keep if off . . .
- If you've got diabetes, high blood pressure, high cholesterol, or heart disease—and you need to re-invent your
  lifestyle . . .
- If you want to raise a healthy family and encourage good
  lifelong habits in your kids . . .

HELP is on the way!

- The Support You Need • The Motivation You Want •
  • A Program That Works •

HELP: Healthy Exchanges Lifetime Plan
is available at your favorite bookstore